200 vegan recipes

hamlyn | all color cookbook

200 vegan recipes

Emma Frost & Nichola Palmer

An Hachette UK Company
www.hachette.co.uk

First published in Great Britain in 2014 by Hamlyn
a division of Octopus Publishing Group Ltd
Endeavour House, 189 Shaftesbury Avenue
London WC2H 8JY
www.octopusbooks.co.uk
www.octopusbooksusa.com

Distributed in the US by
Hachette Book Group
1290 Avenue of the Americas, 4th and 5th Floors
New York, NY 10020

Distributed in Canada by
Canadian Manda Group
664 Annette Street
Toronto, Ontario, Canada M6S 2C8

Some of the recipes in this book have previously appeared
in other titles published by Hamlyn.

ISBN: 978-060062-982-5

Printed and bound in China

10 9 8 7 6 5 4 3 2 1

Standard level spoon and cup measurements
are used in all recipes.

Ovens should be preheated to the specified temperature—
if using a convection oven, follow the manufacturer's
instructions for adjusting the time and temperature.

Fresh herbs should be used unless otherwise stated.
Medium eggs should be used unless otherwise stated.
Freshly ground black pepper should be used unless
otherwise stated

The U.S. Food and Drug Administration advises that eggs
should not be consumed raw. This book contains some dishes
made with raw or lightly cooked eggs. It is prudent for
vulnerable people, such as pregnant and nursing mothers,
people with weakened immune systems, the elderly, babies,
and young children, to avoid uncooked or lightly cooked dishes
made with eggs. Once prepared, these dishes should be kept
refrigerated and used promptly.

contents

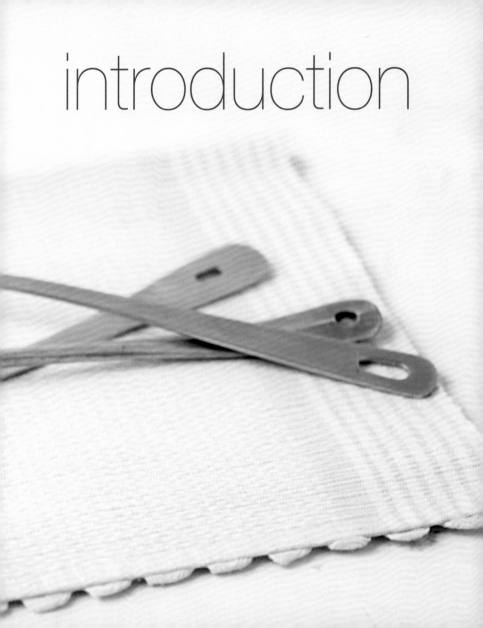

introduction

introduction

Eating a diet that is totally plant based, without animal foods or by-products, has never been easier and is no longer the quirky preference of only those living an alternative lifestyle. Most major supermarkets and main street health-food stores sell a good selection of dairy-free milks, creams, and spreads as well as seeds and whole grains, so all the ingredients you need can be incorporated into your normal shopping routine.

If you are contemplating becoming vegan, have been vegan for years, or will be cooking for a vegan friend or member of the family, whatever your situation, we hope you find inspiration in these easy recipes for every occasion. Being free from animal products, these recipes are also suitable for those with a dairy and/or egg intolerance or allergy.

Eating a healthy vegan diet

More and more of us are turning to a vegan diet, whether on the grounds of personal health or animal welfare, and it can be something you can introduce and adopt gradually. You may want to start with one week a month and then increase your vegan eating pattern over a period of time to reach a level that you are comfortable with, or you may be happy to become completely vegan from the start. You may also find it a good weight-loss diet—a diet rich in whole grains and fiber from fruit and vegetables will keep you feeling fuller for longer with less temptation to snack between meals.

The key to a healthy vegan diet is to eat a variety of foods, including fruit, vegetables, leafy greens, whole grains, nuts, seeds, and legumes (beans), to make every plateful of food a colorful one, which will indicate you are well on the way to achieving a good balance of nutrients.

A vegan diet is not without treats—just turn to the Breads and Baking section (see page 172) and also the Desserts section (see page 202) for a range of delicious breads, cakes, muffins, cookies, and other desserts.

The main nutrients for a healthy vegan diet are found in the following foods:

Protein

Soy is the best source of protein, containing all the essential amino acids needed by the body. Tofu, made from fermented soybeans, is a good meat substitute and can be cooked in stews and stir-fries, marinated and broiled, as well as crumbled to make a decent replacement for scrambled eggs. Other good sources of protein are peas, edamame (soybeans), peanuts, chickpeas, grains such as quinoa (pronounced keenwa) and wheat, nuts, and seeds.

Vitamin B_{12}

Found in yeast extract and often added to breakfast cereals and plant milks.

Calcium

Added to plant milks and found in green vegetables, whole grains, and bread.

Vitamin D

Needed for the absorption of calcium; your body makes its own vitamin D from sunlight, so it is important to get outdoors for a walk every day if possible, but vitamin D is also added to dairy-free spreads.

Iron

Good sources are lentils, tofu, kidney beans, chickpeas, quinoa, and dried fruits, such as dried apricots and figs and prunes.

Omega-3 fatty acids

Usually found in oily fish, but plant sources are leafy green vegetables, nuts, and oils, such as flaxseed, olive, avocado, peanut, and canola.

Frozen vegetables are a great time-saver, prepared and chopped ready to use, and because they are frozen within hours of picking, they often contain more vitamins than fresh, especially if the latter are a few days old.

Fresh herbs provide instant color to cooked grains, freshness to salads, and flavor to salad dressing and sauces. Grow your own if you can, because they are so much cheaper and are there on hand whenever you need them. They don't take up much space—even a windowsill will do. Just keep them well watered and they will last a long time. If you do buy them in packages, any leftovers can be chopped and frozen in ice cube trays topped up with water or oil. Just pop them out and add straight into the pan as you need them.

Making life easier

Keeping a well-stocked pantry with a variety of canned beans and tomatoes, whole grains, seeds, nuts, and oils, and a freezer of vegetables and fruits will help you to maintain healthy eating habits with little effort.

The cost of nuts, seeds, and oils can all add up, so make sure you keep track of the expiration dates, because the oils in all these products will deteriorate and turn rancid after a while. If you buy in bulk, nuts and seeds can be frozen to keep them fresh. Toasting nuts and seeds in a dry skillet will refresh them and bring out their flavor.

Canned beans and tomatoes have a long shelf life and have as much nutritional value as dried (beans) and fresh (tomatoes), so keep a good supply for rustling up a quick chili, soup, or pasta sauce.

Vegan alternatives

There are a lot of options to choose from when looking for nonanimal-base alternatives to cooking and serving staples, so take the opportunity to explore and experiment to find which you like best for different uses.

Milk

There is a wealth of different dairy-free milks available in both chilled and long-life forms including soy, almond, hazelnut, coconut, rice, and oat. The choice mainly comes down to personal taste and flavor preference as well as any intolerances or allergies, such as nut, you may have.

Some plant milks come in sweetened and unsweetened versions, so check the label before you buy—if it doesn't state unsweetened on the packaging, it is usually sweetened. Coconut milk with its mild coconutty flavor is ideal for making rice pudding and for creamy-style casseroles. Rice milk is one of the thinner milks with a light flavor, good for pouring over cereals and making coffee, but one of the least stable when heated.

Nut, soy, and oat milks are good for baking and cooking, because they add a creamy richness to muffins, cakes, and sauces.

Cream

Nondairy cream is usually made from soy, oats, coconut, or nuts, and just as in the dairy versions, they are richer than the milks. They are good for pouring over desserts and for making creamy sauces for pasta, pies, custard, and ice cream.

Cheese

Made from blends of potato starch, vegetable oil, and soy protein, dairy-free cheeses are available in mozzarella, cheddar and Parmesan styles. Keep grated dairy-free mozzarella on hand for sprinkling over pizzas, pasta

casseroles, and baked potatoes. Dairy-free cheeses are not so readily available in supermarkets, so a visit to a health-food store or online Web site is required to source them.

Cooking fats and oils

Whey and buttermilk are often used in spreads made from olive oil and sunflower oil, so check that they are completely dairy-free before buying. Virgin coconut oil, which is

solid at room temperature, is a healthy oil to use for baking and frying, as is canola oil and sunflower oil. Extra virgin olive oil and avocado oil are delicious for drizzling over roasted vegetables and for making salad dressings.

Yogurt

Soy yogurt is the most widely available dairy-free yogurt in a choice of plain and vanilla- and fruit-flavored versions. Plain is great for topping breakfast granola or for making dips, such as Greek-style tzatziki with garlic, mint, and cucumber, to serve as a snack with raw vegetable sticks and whole-wheat pita breads or with spicy foods as a cooling relish.

Honey

Because honey is a by-product from bees, it isn't suitable for a vegan diet. A good alternative is agave nectar, a plant-base syrup, which is also sweeter than honey, so you can use less. Drizzle it straight from the squeezy jar over oatmeal or pancakes, or use in cooking. Maple syrup is another delicious alternative to honey with a slight caramel flavor, making it perfect for desserts and cookies.

Eggs

You may think that cooking without eggs rules out cakes, muffins, pancakes, and mayonnaise in your life, but amazingly it doesn't. It is possible to buy egg substitute from health-food stores, but for the recipes in this book, eggs have been replaced with cider vinegar or

a vegan diet. Grains such as quinoa, bulgur wheat, barley, and spelt add a nutty flavor and plenty of texture to dishes such as risottos and salads and stuffings for vegetables. They are also an easy way to thicken soups and stews for a more substantial meal.

Protein-packed lentils make rich, warming casseroles and soups as well as salads and side dishes. Brown and green lentils tend to retain their shape when cooked and so are good for salads and stuffings, whereas red split lentils cook to a softer puree and therefore make an ideal thickener for soups and stews, and are used for making dhal.

Seeds

They may be tiny but seeds are packed with protein, fiber, iron, vitamins, and omega-3 fatty acids, which means that they are well

lemon juice in cakes and muffins and baking powder in pancakes. You will be surprised how delicious they are and easy to make. For a creamy mayonnaise-style salad dressing, you can use silken tofu blended with lemon juice or a little vinegar.

Wholesome vegan options

Given that grains, legumes, and seeds are a vital source of protein in a vegan diet, it makes sense to make the best of their considerable potential.

Whole grains and lentils

Whole grains contain more iron and B vitamins than refined ones, and are richer in fiber and protein, so they are a preferable choice for

worth generously sprinkling over salads, rice dishes, risottos, and breakfast cereals and mixing into bread dough and muffin mixes. Chia, sesame, pumpkin, sunflower, hemp, and flaxseed are all great nutrition and flavor boosters.

Checking food labels

When shopping, look for products with labels or logos that state that they are suitable for vegans on the packaging. If you are unsure whether an item is vegan, check the ingredients list for any of the following, in which case the product will be unsuitable: Gelatin (made from animal bones), honey, whey (liquid left after milk has been curdled), cochineal (a pink coloring made from crushed insects), textured soy protein products (which are suitable for vegetarians but not vegans, because it usually contains egg), Worcestershire sauce (contains anchovies), Thai fish sauce (made from fermented fish and shellfish), Thai curry paste (usually contains Thai fish sauce), ghee (clarified butter) in Indian-style sauces and naan

"Hidden" nonvegan ingredients

The following products need a careful ingredients check, because some are suitable vegan choices but others are not:
Pasta, especially fresh pasta—check that it is egg free
Noodles—avoid egg noodles and choose rice noodles instead

Dark chocolate—may contain some milk
Beers, wines, and hard cider—some are filtered using animal products
Vegetarian burgers and sausages—may contain eggs, milk, or textured soy protein
Candies and marshmallows—often made with gelatin
Cereal bars and breakfast cereals—may be sweetened with honey

breakfasts &
brunches

mango & orange smoothie

Serves **2**
Preparation time **10 minutes**

1 ripe **mango**, peeled, pitted,
   and chopped, or 1 cup
   frozen **mango chunks**
⅔ cup **plain soy yogurt**
⅔ cup **orange juice**
finely grated zest and juice
   of 1 **lime**
2 teaspoons **agave nectar**,
   or to taste

Blend together the mango, yogurt, orange juice, lime zest and juice, and agave nectar in a blender or food processor until smooth.

Pour into 2 glasses and serve.

For ginger banana smoothie, blend together 1 ripe banana, ¾ inch piece of fresh ginger root, peeled and grated, ⅔ cup plain soy yogurt, and ⅔ cup orange or mango juice in a blender or food processor until smooth. Sweeten to taste with agave nectar, pour into 2 glasses, and serve.

toasted muesli with coconut chips

Serves **8**
Preparation time **15 minutes**
Cooking time **15–20 minutes**

4 cups **rolled oats**
1 cup **coconut chips**
½ cup **sunflower seeds**
1 cup **pumpkin seeds**
1½ cups **slivered almonds**
⅔ cup **hazelnuts**
¼ cup **maple syrup**
2 tablespoons **sunflower oil**
1⅔ cups **golden raisins**
⅔ cup coarsely chopped
   dried figs

To serve
soy milk
raspberries

Mix together the oats, coconut chips, sunflower and pumpkin seeds, slivered almonds, and hazelnuts in a large bowl.

Transfer half the muesli mixture to a separate bowl. Mix the maple syrup and oil together in a small bowl, then pour it over the remaining half of the muesli and toss really well to lightly coat all the ingredients.

Line a large roasting pan with parchment paper, sprinkle with the syrup-coated muesli, and spread out in a single layer. Bake in a preheated oven, at 300°F, for 15–20 minutes, stirring occasionally, until golden and crisp.

Let cool completely, then toss with the uncooked muesli and the dried fruit. Store in airtight storage jars. Serve with soy milk and raspberries.

For soft cinnamon muesli with almonds & banana,

mix together 4 cups rolled oats, 1⅔ cups golden raisins, 1 cup pumpkin seeds, 2 cups toasted blanched almonds, 1½ cups dried banana slices, ½ cup pitted dried dates, ½ cup sunflower seeds, and 2 teaspoons ground cinnamon in a large bowl. Store in airtight storage jars. Serve with soy milk or soy yogurt and fresh fruit, if desired.

mushroom tofu scramble

Serves **4**
Preparation time **15 minutes**
Cooking time **5 minutes**

2 tablespoons **canola** or
  olive oil
3 cups trimmed and quartered
  cremini mushrooms
8 oz **firm tofu**, drained, patted
  dry and crumbled
8 **baby plum tomatoes**,
  halved
1 tablespoon **mushroom**
  ketchup
3 tablespoons chopped **flat**
  leaf parsley
salt and **black pepper**
hash browns, to serve

Heat the oil in a skillet, add the mushrooms, and cook over high heat, stirring frequently, for 2 minutes, until browned and softened. Add the tofu and cook, stirring, for 1 minute.

Add the tomatoes to the pan and cook for 2 minutes, until starting to soften. Stir in the ketchup and half the parsley, then season with salt and black pepper.

Serve immediately with hash browns, sprinkled with the remaining parsley.

For spinach & corn tofu scramble, heat 2 tablespoons canola or olive oil in a skillet. Add 8 oz firm tofu, drained, patted dry and crumbled, with 1 teaspoon smoked paprika and cook, stirring, for 2 minutes, until hot. Add ½ cup frozen or drained canned corn kernels and heat through for 1 minute, then add 8 cups spinach and heat until just wilted. Season with salt and black pepper and serve with hash browns or toasted sourdough bread.

carrot & apple muffins

Makes **12**
Preparation time **20 minutes**
Cooking time **15–20 minutes**

2⅓ cups **all-purpose flour**
2¼ teaspoons **baking powder**
1½ teaspoons **baking soda**
½ teaspoon **salt**
1½ teaspoons **ground cinnamon**
1 teaspoon **ground ginger**
½ cup **raisins**
⅔ cup firmly packed **light brown sugar**
1 tablespoon **poppy seeds**
1 cup **almond milk**
½ cup **olive oil**, plus extra for oiling (optional)
1 tablespoon **cider vinegar**
1 **sweet, crisp apple**, cored and coarsely grated
1 **carrot**, peeled and shredded

Line 12 sections of a muffin pan with paper liners or lightly oil and line the bottoms with disks of parchment paper.

Sift together the flour, baking powder, baking soda, salt, cinnamon, and ginger into a medium mixing bowl. Stir in the raisins, sugar, and poppy seeds.

Mix together the almond milk, oil, and vinegar in a small bowl. Add to the dry ingredients and lightly stir together until just mixed. Quickly fold in the apple and carrot, then divide the batter among the paper liners or the sections of the muffin pan.

Bake immediately in a preheated oven, at 375°F, for 15–20 minutes, until well risen and golden. Transfer to a wire rack to cool. Store the muffins for up to for 2–3 days in an airtight container, or freeze.

For carrot, pine nut & orange muffins, prepare a muffin pan as above. Sift 2⅔ cups all-purpose flour, 2¼ teaspoons baking powder, 1½ teaspoons baking soda, and ½ teaspoon salt together into a bowl. Stir in ⅓ cup toasted pine nuts, ⅔ cup firmly packed light brown sugar, and the finely grated zest of 1 orange. Mix together 1 cup almond milk, ½ cup olive oil, and 1 tablespoon cider vinegar in a small bowl. Add to the dry ingredients and lightly stir together until just mixed. Quickly fold in 2 peeled and shredded carrots, then spoon the batter into the paper liners or muffin sections and bake in a preheated oven, at 375°F, for 15–20 minutes, until well risen and golden. Transfer to a wire rack to cool.

potato bread with tomatoes

Serves **4**

Preparation time **30 minutes**,
   plus proving and cooling

Cooking time about **1 hour**

3 **russet potatoes**, peeled
   and cut into chunks

1 teaspoon **active dry yeast**

1 teaspoon **sugar**

1 tablespoon **sunflower oil**,
   plus extra for oiling

1½ cups **white bread flour**,
   plus extra for dusting

¾ cup **whole-wheat flour**

2 tablespoons chopped
   rosemary

1 tablespoon **thyme leaves**

salt and **black pepper**

Topping

2 tablespoons **olive oil**

1¾ cups halved red, yellow,
   and/or orange **cherry or
   grape tomatoes**

½ teaspoon **thyme leaves**

½ teaspoon **sea salt flakes**

Cook the potatoes in a large saucepan of lightly salted boiling water for 15–20 minutes, until tender but not flaky. Drain really well, reserving the cooking liquid.

Put ⅓ cup of the cooking liquid into a large bowl and let cool until lukewarm. Sprinkle the yeast over the liquid, then stir in the sugar and set aside for 10 minutes.

Mash the potatoes with the oil, then stir in the yeast mixture and mix well with a wooden spoon. Mix in the flours, herbs, and salt and black pepper, turn out onto a lightly floured surface, and knead well to incorporate the last of the flour. Knead the dough until soft and pliable, then put in a lightly oiled bowl, cover with plastic wrap and let rise in a warm place for 1 hour, until well risen.

Knead the dough on a lightly floured surface, then coarsely shape into a round, place on a baking sheet, and lightly cover with oiled plastic wrap. Let rise in a warm place for 30 minutes. Score a cross into the dough with a knife and bake in a preheated oven, at 425°F, for 35–40 minutes, until well risen and crusty on top. Transfer to a wire rack to cool for 30 minutes.

Cut 4 slices of the bread and lightly toast. Meanwhile, heat the oil for the topping in a skillet, add the tomatoes, and cook over high heat for 2–3 minutes, until softened. Stir in the thyme and salt flakes. Serve with the toasted bread, seasoned with black pepper.

For sweet potato & onion seed bread, prepare the dough as above, using 3 small sweet potatoes, peeled and chopped, in place of the potato and boiling for 8–10 minutes, until just tender, and 2 tablespoons onion seeds instead of the herbs. Bake as above.

almond, raspberry & date bars

Makes **12**
Preparation time **10 minutes**
Cooking time **15 minutes**

⅓ cup **chunky almond butter**
½ cup **agave syrup**
¼ cup **soy margarine**
¼ cup **demerara** or **other raw sugar**
1⅔ cups **rolled oats**
2 tablespoons **rice flour**
½ teaspoon **ground cinnamon**
1 cup pitted and chopped fresh **Medjool dates**
1 cup **raspberries**
¼ cup coarsely chopped **walnuts**
1 teaspoon **sesame seeds**
1 tablespoon **sunflower seeds**
sunflower oil, for oiling

Heat the almond butter, agave syrup, vegan margarine, and demerara sugar in a saucepan over low heat, stirring constantly, until melted. Add the oats, flour, cinnamon, and dates and mix well.

Transfer the batter to a lightly oiled 7 x 11 inch shallow baking pan and level with the back of a metal spoon, slightly dampened to ease spreading. With a teaspoon, make holes in the batter and press in the raspberries, then sprinkle with the walnuts, sesame seeds, and sunflower seeds. Bake in a preheated oven, at 375°F, for 15 minutes, or until the edges turn a pale golden brown.

Let cool in the pan for 10 minutes before scoring into 12 bars, then let cool completely before cutting into bars and carefully removing from the pan.

For peanut butter, banana & raisin oat bars,
prepare the batter as above, replacing the almond butter with ⅓ cup chunky peanut butter and using 1 large banana, finely chopped, instead of the dates. Stir ¼ cup jumbo raisins into the batter before baking and then cooling, scoring, and cutting into squares as above.

plum, banana & apple crisps

Serves **4**
Preparation time **15 minutes**
Cooking time **30 minutes**

6 **plums**, halved and pitted
¼ cup **vegan margarine**
2 **crisp, sweet apples**, peeled,
    cored, and cut into chunks
2 tablespoons **demerara** or
    other raw sugar
2 **bananas**, cut into chunks
½ teaspoon **ground
    cinnamon**
pinch of **ground allspice**
    (optional)

Crumb topping
¾ cup **all-purpose flour**
¼ cup **vegan margarine**,
    cubed
¼ cup **demerara** or **other
    raw sugar**
¼ cup **rolled oats**

Cook the plums with the vegan margarine in a saucepan over gentle heat for 3 minutes. Add the apples and demerara sugar and cook, stirring occasionally, for another 2–3 minutes.

Remove the pan from the heat, add the bananas and spices, and toss gently to lightly coat all the fruit in the sugar and spice. Divide the batter among four 1-cup gratin dishes.

Put the flour for the crumb topping in a bowl, add the spread, and rub in with the fingertips until the mixture resembles fine bread crumbs. Stir in the sugar and oats. Spoon evenly over the top of the fruit in each dish, place the dishes on a baking sheet, and bake in a preheated oven, at 400°F, for 20 minutes, until the topping is golden and the fruit is bubbling. Serve with plain soy yogurt, if desired.

For prune & banana crisps, put 2 cups pitted prunes into a saucepan with 1 tablespoon demerara or other raw sugar, ½ teaspoon ground cinnamon, and ⅔ cup water. Bring to a boil, then cover and simmer for 3 minutes. Remove from the heat and stir in 2 sliced bananas. Divide among the dishes, top with the crumb mixture, and bake as above. Serve with plain soy yogurt.

home-baked beans on toast

Serves **4**
Preparation time **10 minutes,**
  plus overnight soaking
Cooking time
  1 hour 20 minutes

1¾ cups **dried navy beans**
2 tablespoons **canola oil**
1 **red onion**, cut into wedges
1 (14½ oz) can **diced
  tomatoes**
2 tablespoons **tomato paste**
2 tablespoons packed **dark
  brown sugar**
3 tablespoons **red wine
  vinegar**
1 teaspoon **paprika**
1 teaspoon **mustard powder**
1 cup **vegetable stock**
salt and **black pepper**
2 tablespoons chopped
  flat leaf parsley, to garnish
whole-wheat toast, to serve

Soak the beans in plenty of cold water overnight. Drain, put into a saucepan, and cover with cold water. Bring to a boil, then drain and return to the pan. Cover with fresh cold water, bring to a boil, and boil for 10 minutes, then cover and simmer for 50 minutes until tender.

Meanwhile, heat the oil in a separate saucepan, add the onion, and sauté for 3 minutes, until just starting to soften. Add the tomatoes, tomato paste, sugar, vinegar, paprika, mustard powder, and stock. Bring to a boil, stirring, then reduce the heat and simmer, uncovered, for 20 minutes, until reduced slightly.

Drain the cooked beans and add to the tomato sauce. Simmer for another 15–20 minutes, covered, until thick, then season with salt and black pepper and serve on whole-wheat toast, sprinkled with the chopped parsley.

For quick chili beans with vegetable sausages, heat 1 (14½ oz) can diced tomatoes in a saucepan with 2 tablespoons tomato paste, 2 tablespoons packed dark brown sugar, 1 tablespoon sweet chili sauce, and 1 chopped red chile. Bring to a boil, stirring, then simmer, uncovered, for 10 minutes. Add 1 drained (14½ oz) can navy beans and simmer for another 10 minutes. Meanwhile, broil or pan-fry 10 oz vegan vegetable sausages. Cut into chunks and stir into the bean mixture. Serve on whole-wheat toast.

cranberry, oat & raisin cookies

Makes **12**
Preparation time **10 minutes**
Cooking time **12–15 minutes**

¼ cup **soy margarine** or other
   vegan spread
⅓ cup **light corn syrup**
1 cup **whole-wheat flour**
¾ cup **rolled oats**
1 teaspoon **baking powder**
½ teaspoon **ground
   cinnamon**
½ teaspoon **ground ginger**
pinch of freshly grated **nutmeg**
⅓ cup **dried cranberries**
⅓ cup **raisins**

Heat the spread with the syrup in a saucepan over low heat, stirring, until melted. Remove from the heat, add the remaining ingredients, and mix well.

Spoon the dough onto a large baking sheet lined with parchment paper into 12 large mounds and press down slightly with the back of a spoon. Bake in a preheated oven, at 350°F, for 8–10 minutes, until the edges are golden but the centers are still soft.

Let cool for 2–3 minutes on the baking sheet before transferring to a wire rack to cool completely.

For chocolate & cherry cookies, melt the spread with the light corn syrup, then remove from the heat, add the flour and rolled oats, and mix well as above. Let cool for 10 minutes, then stir in 3 oz coarsely chopped semisweet chocolate and ⅓ cup dried cherries. Form into 12 mounds and bake as above.

creamy mushrooms with walnuts

Serves **2**
Preparation time **10 minutes**
Cooking time **8 minutes**

1 tablespoon **olive oil**
2 cups trimmed and sliced
  cremini mushrooms
1 **garlic clove**, crushed
2 **thyme sprigs**, plus extra
  to garnish
⅔ cup **soy** or **oat cream**
1 teaspoon **soy sauce**
½ cup **chopped walnuts**,
  toasted
black pepper
bagels, halved and toasted

Heat the oil in a skillet, add the mushrooms, and cook over high heat, stirring frequently, for 2 minutes, until browned and softened.

Reduce the heat and add the garlic, thyme, soy or oat cream, and soy sauce. Simmer, stirring, for 3 minutes, adding a little water if the sauce is too thick. Stir in the walnuts and season with black pepper (the soy sauce is salty, so you won't need to season with salt).

Spoon the mushroom mixture over the toasted bagels and garnish with thyme sprigs before serving.

For creamy kale with sun-dried tomatoes, heat 1 tablespoon olive oil in a skillet, add 1 crushed garlic clove and 3 cups shredded kale, and cook over medium-high heat, stirring, for 5 minutes, until the kale is just tender. Add ⅔ cup coconut milk or cream and 1 teaspoon soy sauce and simmer, stirring, for 2 minutes, adding a little water if the sauce is too thick. Stir in ½ cup chopped, drained sun-dried tomatoes in oil and season with black pepper. Heat for 1 minute, then spoon over halved and toasted bagels to serve.

appetizers, snacks & soups

tapenade bruschetta

Makes **12**
Preparation time **15 minutes**
Cooking time **10 minutes**

1 small **ciabatta loaf**, cut into
   12 slices
3 tablespoons **olive oil**
1 **garlic clove**, crushed
1 tablespoon chopped
   flat leaf parsley
12 **marinated sun-dried**
   tomatoes in oil, drained

Tapenade
1½ cups **pitted black**
   ripe olives
1 **garlic clove**
small handful of **flat leaf**
   parsley
2 tablespoons **capers**
1 tablespoon **lemon juice**
2 tablespoons **olive oil**
salt and **black pepper**

Arrange the ciabatta slices in a single layer on a baking sheet. Mix the oil, garlic, and chopped parsley together and brush over the bread slices. Bake in a preheated oven, at 400°F, for 10 minutes, until golden and crisp.

Meanwhile, put the olives, garlic, parsley, capers, lemon juice, and oil in a food processor and process to a coarse paste. Season with salt and black pepper.

Spread the tapenade over the toasts and top each with a sun-dried tomato.

For artichoke tapenade bruschetta, toast the ciabatta slices as above. Meanwhile, put ¾ cup pitted green olives and 1 cup drained, marinated artichokes in oil (reserving 2 tablespoons of the oil), a small handful of flat leaf parsley, 2 tablespoons capers, 1 garlic clove, 1 tablespoon lemon juice, and the reserved artichoke oil in a food processor and process to a coarse paste. Season with salt and black pepper. Spread the tapenade over the toasts and sprinkle with chopped parsley.

summer vegetable tempura

Serves **4**

Preparation time **20 minutes**

Cooking time **15 minutes**

vegetable oil, for deep-frying

⅔ cup **all-purpose flour**

2 tablespoons **cornstarch**

pinch of **salt**

1 cup ice-cold
   sparkling water

1 **red bell pepper**, cored,
   seeded, and cut into strips

12 thin **asparagus spears**,
   trimmed

1 **zucchini**, trimmed and sliced

Dipping sauce

2 tablespoons **sweet
   chili sauce**

2 tablespoons **soy sauce**

1 teaspoon finely grated
   lemon zest

1 tablespoon **lemon juice**

Mix the dipping sauce ingredients together in a serving bowl and set aside.

Fill a deep saucepan halfway with vegetable oil and heat to 350–375°F, or until a cube of bread dropped into the oil browns in 30 seconds. Just before the oil is hot enough, using a wire whisk, quickly beat together the flour, cornstarch, salt, and sparkling water in a bowl to make a slightly lumpy batter.

Dip one-third of the vegetables into the batter until coated and then drop straight into the hot oil. Fry for 2 minutes, until crisp. Remove from the pan with a slotted spoon, drain on paper towels, and keep warm in a low oven.

Fry the remaining vegetables in 2 more batches. Serve hot with the dipping sauce.

For broccoli & mushroom tempura with sesame dipping sauce, mix together 3 tablespoons soy sauce, 1 tablespoon sesame oil, the juice of 1 lime, and 1 finely chopped scallion in a serving bowl for a dipping sauce and set aside. Make the batter as above. Dip 3½ cups broccoli florets and 3 cups trimmed button mushrooms into the batter to coat and deep-fry, in batches, as above. Serve hot with the sesame dipping sauce.

fava bean & herb crostini

Makes **12**
Preparation time **20 minutes**
Cooking time **15 minutes**

1⅔ cups shelled **fava beans**
  (you will need double this
  quantity if buying in the pod)
2 tablespoons chopped **mint**
1 tablespoon chopped **flat
  leaf parsley**
finely grated zest of **1 lemon**
2 **scallions**, finely chopped
1 **garlic clove**, crushed
12 slices of **French bread**
2 tablespoons **chili oil**
salt and **black pepper**
arugula, to garnish
lemon wedges, to serve

Cook the fava beans in a saucepan of boiling water for 3 minutes. Drain, rinse under cold water, and drain again. Pop the beans out of the outer skins and put in a bowl.

Crush the beans lightly with a potato masher, then stir in the mint, parsley, lemon zest, scallions, and garlic. Season with salt and black pepper.

Heat a ridged grill pan or skillet until hot. Brush the bread slices with the chili oil, add to the hot pan, in batches, and cook for 1 minute, until toasted and crisp. Turn and cook on the other side for 1 minute.

Spoon the fava bean mixture onto the toasts, garnish with arugula, and serve with lemon wedges for squeezing over the top.

For fava bean, cilantro & cumin crostini,
cook the fava beans as above, then peel and place in a bowl. Toast 1 tablespoon cumin seeds in a dry skillet over medium heat, shaking the pan occasionally, until starting to smell fragrant and then add to the beans. Lightly crush the beans and cumin together with a potato masher. Stir in 2 tablespoons chopped cilantro, ½ finely chopped green chile, and 1 tablespoon lemon juice. Season with salt and black pepper. Toast the French bread slices as above, then spoon on the fava bean mixture and garnish with thinly sliced red onion and cilantro leaves.

avocado & cucumber sushi

Serves **4**

Preparation time **20 minutes**,
plus standing/steaming

Cooking time **15 minutes**

1 cup **sushi rice**

¼ cup **rice vinegar**

2 tablespoons **granulated
sugar**

2 tablespoons **sesame seeds**,
toasted

4 sheets of **nori seaweed**

1 small **avocado**, peeled,
pitted, and cut into slim
wedges

¼ **cucumber**, cut into long
thin sticks

To serve

soy sauce

wasabi

pickled ginger

Cook and let the rice stand/steam according to the package directions, then transfer to a bowl.

Put the vinegar and sugar in a cup and microwave for 30 seconds, until hot. Pour into the cooked rice and mix well—the rice should be sticky. Stir in the sesame seeds.

Lay out the sheets of nori seaweed and divide the rice among them. Spread evenly to the edges, then arrange the avocado wedges and cucumber strips across the length of the rice in the bottom third of each sheet. Starting at the filled end, gently roll the each nori sheet up tightly until a neat roll is formed, brushing with a little water to hold the seaweed tightly in place.

Use a sharp knife to slice the rolls into 1 inch-thick pieces. Serve with soy sauce and wasabi for dipping, along with some pickled ginger.

For asparagus & red pepper rolls, cook 8 trimmed asparagus spears and ½ red bell pepper, cored, seeded, and cut into strips, in a saucepan of salted boiling water for 2 minutes, until just tender, then immediately remove with a slotted spoon to a colander, rinse with cold water, and drain. Set aside on paper towels to cool. Cook and let the sushi rice stand/steam as above, then use the asparagus and red bell pepper in place of the avocado and cucumber to prepare 4 nori rolls as above. Slice and serve as above.

eggplant dip & crispy tortillas

Serves **6**
Preparation time **15 minutes**,
  plus cooling
Cooking time **30 minutes**

1 **large eggplant** (about
  1 ½ lb), trimmed and cut
  into thick chunks
½ cup **extra virgin olive oil**
1 **garlic clove**, crushed
½ teaspoon **smoked paprika**
3 tablespoons **tahini**
juice of 1 **lemon**
1 tablespoon chopped
  flat leaf parsley
salt and **black pepper**

Tortillas
6 mini **flour tortillas**, cut into
  triangles
1 tablespoon **olive oil**
1 teaspoon **sea salt flakes**

Put the eggplant in a bowl with ⅓ cup of the extra virgin olive oil and toss well. Transfer to a large roasting pan and roast in a preheated oven, at 425°F, for 25 minutes, until soft and lightly charred in places. Let cool.

Transfer the eggplant to a food processor and add the garlic, ¼ teaspoon of the smoked paprika, the tahini, lemon juice, half the chopped parsley, and plenty of salt and black pepper. Process until smooth, then transfer to a serving bowl.

Mix the remaining extra virgin olive oil with the remaining paprika and use to swirl over the top of the dip. Sprinkle with the remaining chopped parsley.

Brush each tortilla triangle lightly with the olive oil and spread out on 1–2 large baking sheets. Sprinkle with the salt and cook under a preheated medium broiler for 1–2 minutes, until lightly crisp and golden. Arrange around the bowl of dip and serve.

For spicy chili, eggplant & red pepper dip, toss a medium eggplant (about 1 lb), trimmed and cut into chunks, and 1 large red bell pepper, cored, seeded, and cut into chunks, with ⅓ cup extra virgin olive oil. Transfer to a roasting pan and roast in a preheated oven, at 425°F, for 25 minutes, until soft and lightly charred. Let cool, then transfer to a food processor with ½ seeded and finely chopped red chile, ¼ cup chopped cilantro, a pinch of salt, and plenty of black pepper and process until smooth. Transfer to a serving bowl, sprinkle with chopped cilantro, and serve with crispy tortillas, prepared as above.

flatbread, roasted veg & hummus

Serves **4**

Preparation time **20 minutes**,
plus standing

Cooking time **20 minutes**

1⅔ cups **whole-wheat flour**,
plus extra for dusting

½ teaspoon **salt**

1 **red bell pepper**, cored,
seeded, and cut into chunks

1 **orange bell pepper**, cored,
seeded, and cut into chunks

1 **green bell pepper**, cored,
seeded, and cut into chunks

1 large **red onion**, cut into thin
wedges

2 tablespoons **olive oil**

½ teaspoon **ground coriander**

½ teaspoon **cumin seeds**

Hummus

1 (15 oz) can **chickpeas**,
drained well

finely grated zest and juice
of 1 **lemon**

3 tablespoons chopped
parsley

1 tablespoon **tahini**

3 tablespoons **olive oil**

salt and **black pepper**

Mix the flour and salt together in a bowl, then add enough water to bring the mixture together into a dough—about ⅓–½ cup. Turn out onto a lightly floured surface and knead well until smooth. Return to the bowl, cover with plastic wrap, and let rest in a warm place for 30 minutes.

Toss the bell peppers and onion with the oil in a large roasting pan, then add the coriander and cumin and toss again. Roast in a preheated oven, at 425°F, for 20 minutes, until softened.

Meanwhile, blend together all the ingredients for the hummus in a blender or food processor until smooth.

Divide the flatbread dough into 4 pieces and roll out each into a 10 inch circle. Heat a large skillet until hot and cook the flatbreads for about 45 seconds on each side until lightly golden, flipping over with a spatula.

Spread each warm flatbread with some of the hummus, then top with one-quarter of the hot roasted vegetables and fold to serve.

For seeded flatbreads with roasted veg & lima bean paste, prepare the flatbread dough as above, mixing 1 tablespoon cumin seeds with the flour and salt. Roast the vegetables as above, omitting the cumin seeds. Blend together 1 well-drained (15 oz) can lima beans, 3 tablespoons olive oil, 1 tablespoon thyme leaves, finely grated zest of 1 lemon, 1 crushed garlic clove, and salt and black pepper in a blender until smooth. Cook the flatbread dough and then serve rolled up with the bean paste and roasted veg as above.

mushroom risotto cakes

Serves **4**
Preparation time **20 minutes**,
  plus cooling
Cooking time **25 minutes**

3 tablespoons **olive oil**
1 **red onion**, finely chopped
1 **leek**, trimmed, cleaned, and
  finely sliced
3½ cups trimmed and
  coarsely chopped **cremini
  mushrooms**
1 **garlic clove**, crushed
1 cup **risotto rice**
2½ cups **vegetable stock**,
  plus extra if needed
⅔ cup **white wine**
½ cup **cornmeal**
¼ cup **sunflower oil**

Heat the olive oil in a large, heavy skillet, add the onion, leek, mushrooms, and garlic, and cook over medium-high heat for 5–6 minutes, until softened and golden in places. Add the rice and stir well, then add the stock and wine, reduce the heat to a gentle simmer, and cook, stirring frequently, until the liquid is almost all absorbed and the rice is tender and cooked through, adding more stock, if necessary.

Remove the pan from the heat and let cool for 20 minutes. The mixture will not only cool but more liquid will be absorbed and the rice will become a little more heavier.

Divide the mixture into 8 and mold each portion into a large patty, then toss liberally in the cornmeal and set aside.

Heat the sunflower oil in a skillet and cook the cakes over medium-high heat for 2–3 minutes on each side until golden and crisp. Serve hot with a simple dressed salad.

For butternut squash risotto cakes, cook the onion and leek over medium-high heat as above with 1½ cups peeled, seeded, and finely chopped butternut squash pieces in place of the mushrooms. Then reduce the heat, cover, and cook for another 3–4 minutes. Remove the lid, add the rice, and continue as above. Serve the cakes with a simple salad.

seeded fries with red pepper dip

Serves **4**

Preparation time **20 minutes**

Cooking time **35 minutes**

3 **sweet potatoes**, peeled and cut into wedges

4 **russet potatoes**, peeled and cut into wedges

¼ cup **olive oil**

1 tablespoon **poppy seeds**

1 tablespoon **sesame seeds**

1 teaspoon **dried red pepper flakes**

1 large **red bell pepper**, cored, seeded, and cut into 4 wedges

2 **tomatoes**, halved

½ teaspoon **smoked paprika**

3 tablespoons **chopped cilantro**

salt and **black pepper**

Drizzle the sweet potato and russet potato wedges with 3 tablespoons of the olive oil in a large roasting pan and toss well, then sprinkle with the poppy and sesame seeds and red pepper flakes and toss again. Season generously with salt and black pepper and roast in the top of a preheated oven, at 400°F, for 35 minutes, until golden.

Meanwhile, put the bell pepper wedges and tomatoes in a smaller roasting pan, then drizzle with the remaining olive oil and toss well. Roast on a lower shelf in the oven for 25 minutes, until softened and lightly charred in places.

Transfer the roasted bell pepper and tomatoes to a food processor, season generously with salt and black pepper and add the smoked paprika. Process until almost smooth but with a little texture still remaining. Spoon into a small serving bowl and place in the center of a serving plate.

Arrange the roasted potato wedges on the plate, sprinkle with the chopped cilantro, and serve.

For parsnip fries with horseradish dip, peel 4 large parsnips, cut each into 8 wedges, and put in a roasting pan. Toss with 3 tablespoons olive oil and roast in a preheated oven, at 400°F, for 25 minutes, until softened and crisp at the edges. Toss with 2 tablespoons maple syrup and 1 tablespoon whole-grain mustard, then arrange on a serving plate and serve with a bowl of horseradish sauce for dipping.

eggplant with caper & mint pesto

Serves **4**
Preparation time **20 minutes**
Cooking time **15 minutes**

2 **eggplants**, trimmed and
  sliced
²⁄₃ cup **extra virgin olive oil**
warm **pita bread,** to serve

Pesto
finely grated zest and juice
  of 1 **lemon**
3 tablespoons **olive oil**
2 tablespoons **red wine
  vinegar**
¼ cup chopped **mint leaves,**
  plus extra leaves to garnish
2 tablespoons **capers,**
  coarsely chopped
1 **garlic clove,** coarsely
  chopped
1 teaspooon **sugar**
salt and **black pepper**

Put the eggplant slices in a large bowl, pour the oil
over them, and toss well, using both hands to coat as
evenly as possible. The oil will be absorbed fast, so work
as quickly as possible. Set aside for 10 minutes while
making the pesto.

Mix all the pesto ingredients together in a small bowl.
Season with a little salt and black pepper.

Heat a ridged grill pan until smoking, then lay several
of the eggplant slices onto the hot pan in a single layer
and cook over high heat for 1–2 minutes on each side,
until lightly charred and soft. Transfer to heatproof
plate and keep warm in a low oven while cooking the
remaining slices.

Drizzle or spoon some of the pesto over the eggplant
slices and serve with warm pita bread, with the
remaining pesto separately.

For warm grilled vegetables with classic pesto, cut
2 red bell peppers into quarters, discarding the cores
and seeds, and put in a large bowl. Add 2 zucchini,
trimmed and sliced lengthwise, and 4 large mushrooms,
trimmed, then pour ⅓ cup olive oil over the vegetables
and toss well. To make the pesto, mix together
¼ cup chopped basil, 3 tablespoons olive oil, and
2 tablespoons each red wine vinegar and lightly toasted
pine nuts, coarsely chopped, in a small bowl. Season
generously with salt and black pepper. Heat a ridged
grill pan until smoking, add the vegetables, in batches,
and cook over high heat for 2–3 minutes on each side,
until lightly charred and soft. Arrange on a serving plate
and drizzle with the pesto to serve.

tomato & thyme tart

Serves **6**
Preparation time **20 minutes**,
　plus chilling
Cooking time **35 minutes**

2 cups **all-purpose flour**, plus
　extra for dusting
½ cup **soy spread**, cubed
¼ cup **thyme leaves**, plus
　extra for garnish
2–3 tablespoons **cold water**
3 tablespoons **olive oil**
1 **onion**, finely chopped
16 red, yellow, and orange
　cherry tomatoes, halved
½ teaspoon **sea salt flakes**
salt and **black pepper**

Put the flour in a bowl and season with salt and black pepper. Add the spread and rub in with the fingertips until the mixture resembles fine bread crumbs. Stir in half the thyme, then add enough of the measured water to bring the mixture together into a firm dough.

Roll the dough out on a lightly floured surface and use to line a 9 inch fluted tart pan. Chill until ready to use.

Heat 1 tablespoon of the oil in a skillet, add the onion, and cook over medium-high heat for 5–6 minutes, until softened and golden. Stir in the remaining thyme leaves and cook for another 1 minute. Spoon the onion mixture into the pastry shell and smooth over.

Toss the tomatoes in a bowl with the remaining oil, the salt flakes, and plenty of black pepper. Arrange on top of the onion in the pastry shell and bake in a preheated oven, at 425°F, for 20–25 minutes, until the pastry is golden and the tomatoes softened and lightly charred in places. Garnish with thyme leaves to serve.

For mixed tomato calzone, make up 1 (6½ oz) package pizza crust mix according to the directions and set aside. Heat 1 tablespoon olive oil in a skillet, add 1 coarsely chopped onion, and cook over medium-high heat for 5–6 minutes, until softened and golden. Toss in a bowl with 10 cherry tomatoes, halved, and 1 tablespoon thyme leaves. Roll out the pizza crust mix on a lightly floured surface into a 10 inch circle and pile the tomato mixture onto one half. Lightly brush the edges with cold water and fold over to seal. Place on a baking sheet and bake in a preheated oven, at 425°F, for 20 minutes, until golden.

pea & pesto soup

Serves **4**
Preparation time **15 minutes**
Cooking time **25 minutes**

1 tablespoon **olive oil**
1 **leek**, trimmed, cleaned,
    and chopped
1 **potato**, peeled and chopped
2⅓ cups **vegetable stock**
2⅓ cups **frozen peas**
salt
ciabatta croutons, to serve

Pesto
⅓ cup **pine nuts**, toasted
2 large handfuls of **basil
    leaves**, plus extra to garnish
1 **garlic clove**
½ cup Parmesan-style or
    cheddar-style **vegan cheese**
½ cup **olive oil**
salt and **black pepper**

Process the pine nuts, basil, garlic, and vegan cheese for the pesto in a food processor until finely chopped. With the motor running, gradually add the oil until blended. Season with salt and black pepper. Set aside.

Heat the oil in a saucepan, add the leek and potato, and cook over gentle heat for 5 minutes, until softened. Add the stock and bring to a boil, then cover and simmer for 10 minutes. Stir in the peas and cook for another 5 minutes, then stir in ¼ cup of the pesto.

Transfer the soup, in batches, to the food processor or a blender and blend until smooth. Return to the pan and reheat, then season with salt and add more pesto, if desired, to taste (the remainder will keep in the refrigerator for several days). Ladle into bowls, spoon over any remaining pesto, garnish with basil leaves, and serve with ciabatta croutons.

For zucchini soup with pesto, prepare the pesto as above (or use store-bought vegan pesto). Heat the oil in a saucepan and add the leek and potato as above with 1 trimmed and chopped zucchini and 1 crushed garlic clove, then cook over gentle heat for 5 minutes, until softened. Add the stock as above and bring to a boil, then cover and simmer for 15 minutes. Stir in ¼ cup pesto and then blend the soup in batches in a food processor or blender until smooth. Reheat, season with salt and black pepper, and add more pesto, if desired, to taste. Garnish with basil leaves and serve with ciabatta croutons.

black bean soup with noodles

Serves **4**

Preparation time **10 minutes**

Cooking time **10 minutes**

2 tablespoons **peanut** or
  vegetable oil

bunch of **scallions**, sliced

2 **garlic cloves**, coarsely
  chopped

1 **red chile,** seeded and sliced

1½ inch piece of **fresh ginger
  root,** peeled and grated

½ cup **black bean sauce** or
  black bean stir-fry sauce

3 cups **vegetable stock**

3 cups shredded **bok choy**
  or **collard greens**

2 teaspoons **soy sauce**

1 teaspoon **sugar**

⅓ cup **raw unsalted peanuts**

8 oz **dried Japanese soba
  noodles**

Heat the oil in a saucepan, add the scallions and garlic, and cook gently for 1 minute.

Add the chile, ginger, black bean sauce, and stock and bring to a boil. Stir in the bok choy or collard greens, soy sauce, sugar, and peanuts, then simmer gently, uncovered, for 4 minutes.

Meanwhile, cook the noodles in a saucepan of boiling water for about 5 minutes, or according to package directions, until just tender.

Drain the noodles and pile into serving bowls. Ladle the soup over the noodles and serve immediately.

For black bean soba nests, cook 8 oz dried Japanese soba noodles as above, drain, and set aside. Meanwhile, heat 1 tablespoon vegetable oil in a wok or large skillet, add a bunch of scallions, coarsely but chunkily chopped, and 1 thinly sliced red chile, and stir-fry over medium-high heat for 1 minute. Add a 1 inch piece of fresh ginger root, peeled and coarsely chopped, and 1 head of bok choy, coarsely sliced, and stir-fry for 1 minute. Add ⅔ cup black bean sauce or black bean stir-fry sauce and heat through until piping hot. Remove from the heat and toss in the cooked noodles. Using 2 forks, twist the noodles into 8 nests and place 2 nests on each of 4 small serving plates, then sprinkle with 3 tablespoons coarsely chopped peanuts and 1 tablespoon chopped cilantro. Serve as an appetizer.

roasted red pepper & lentil soup

Serves **4**
Preparation time **20 minutes**
Cooking time **45 minutes**

2 **red bell peppers**, quartered,
    cored, and seeded
1 **red onion**, cut into wedges
1 tablespoon **olive oil**
3 **garlic cloves**, unpeeled
1 cup **dried red split lentils**,
    rinsed and drained
1 teaspoon **dried red**
    pepper flakes
1 teaspoon **ground cumin**
4 cups **vegetable stock**
2 tablespoons **mixed seeds**,
    such as pumpkin, sunflower,
    sesame, and flaxseed,
    toasted
salt and **black pepper**
coarsely chopped **cilantro**,
    to garnish

Put the bell peppers and onion on a baking sheet. Drizzle with the oil, season with salt and black pepper, and toss until evenly coated in the oil, then spread out in a single layer. Roast in a preheated oven, at 400°F, for 20 minutes, turning once and adding the garlic cloves halfway through, until the bell peppers are starting to char and the onions are soft.

Squeeze the garlic out of its skin and put into a saucepan. Add the roasted bell peppers to the pan with the onion and any oil from the baking sheet. Add the lentils, red pepper flakes, cumin, and stock. Bring to a boil, cover, and simmer for 20 minutes, until the lentils are soft.

Transfer the soup, in batches, to a blender or food processor and blend until smooth. Return to the pan and reheat through. Ladle into bowls, sprinkle with the toasted seeds, and garnish with chopped cilantro.

For roasted tomato, lentil & basil soup, spread out 8 halved tomatoes (about 2 lb) in a roasting pan, drizzle with 2 tablespoons olive oil, and season with salt and black pepper. Roast in a preheated oven, at 400°F, for 10 minutes, then add 3 unpeeled garlic cloves and roast for 10 minutes, until soft. Squeeze the garlic out of its skin into a saucepan. Add the tomatoes, removing as much of the skins as possible, and any juices from the pan with 1 cup rinsed dried red split lentils, 2 tablespoons tomato paste, 1 teaspoon dried red pepper flakes, a handful of basil leaves, and 4 cups vegetable stock. Bring to a boil, cover, and simmer for 20 minutes, until the lentils are soft. Blend the soup, in batches, in a blender or food processor until smooth, then reheat, ladle into bowls, and garnish with basil leaves.

tomato & balsamic vinegar soup

Serves **6**
Preparation time **25 minutes**
Cooking time **20 minutes**

4 large **tomatoes**
2 tablespoons **olive oil**
1 **onion**, coarsely chopped
1 **large baking potato**,
   peeled and diced
2 **garlic cloves**, finely chopped
   (optional)
3 cups **vegetable stock**
1 tablespoon **tomato paste**
1 tablespoon packed **dark
   brown sugar**
4 teaspoons **balsamic vinegar**
small bunch of **basil**
salt and **black pepper**

Cut the tomatoes in half, place them cut side down in an aluminum foil-lined broiler pan, and drizzle with some of the oil. Broil for 4–5 minutes under a preheated broiler until the skins have split and blackened.

Meanwhile, heat the remaining oil in a saucepan, add the onion, potato, and garlic, if using, and cook for 5 minutes, stirring occasionally until softened and turning golden around the edges.

Remove the skins from the tomatoes and coarsely chop the flesh, then add to the onion and potato with any juices from the broiler pan, then stir in the stock, tomato paste, sugar, and vinegar. Add half the basil, season with salt and black pepper, and bring to a boil, then cover and simmer for 15 minutes.

Transfer half the soup to a blender or food processor and blend until smooth. Return to the pan with the remainder of the soup and reheat. Season to taste, then ladle into bowls, garnish with the remaining basil leaves, and serve with Parmesan-style vegan cheese pastry twists, if desired.

spicy cilantro & lentil soup

Serves **8**
Preparation time
10–15 minutes
Cooking time **about**
50 minutes

2 tablespoons **vegetable oil**
2 **onions**, chopped
2 **garlic cloves**, chopped
2 **celery sticks**, chopped
2½ cups **dried red split lentils**, rinsed and drained
1 (14½ oz) **can diced tomatoes**, drained
1 **chile**, seeded and chopped (optional)
1 teaspoon **paprika**
1 teaspoon **harissa**
1 teaspoon **ground cumin**
5 cups **vegetable stock**
salt and **black pepper**
2 tablespoons chopped **cilantro**, to garnish

Heat the oil in a large saucepan, add the onions, garlic, and celery, and cook over gentle heat for a few minutes, until softened.

Stir the lentils into the pan with the tomatoes. Add the chile, if using, paprika, harissa, cumin, and stock and season with salt and black pepper.

Bring to a boil, then cover and simmer gently for 40–50 minutes, until the lentils are tender, adding a little more stock or water if the soup gets too thick. Serve garnished with the chopped cilantro.

For spicy cilantro & white bean soup, cook the onions, garlic, and celery in the oil as above. Drain 2 (15 oz) cans navy or cannellini beans, then add to the pan with the chile, flavorings, and stock as above. Simmer for 40–50 minutes, then coarsely mash some of the beans to thicken the soup. Stir in 2 tablespoons chopped cilantro and ¼ cup chopped parsley to finish.

butternut soup with peanut pesto

Serves **6**
Preparation time **20 minutes**
Cooking time **40 minutes**

2 tablespoons **olive oil**
1 **onion**, finely chopped
1 **butternut squash**, peeled,
seeded, and cut into chunks
1⅔ cups **coconut milk**
1 tablespoon vegan **Thai
green curry paste**
2½ cups **vegetable stock**

Pesto
1 **green chile**, seeded and
finely chopped
2 tablespoons **peanuts**,
coarsely chopped
¼ cup chopped **cilantro**
½ inch piece of **fresh ginger
root**, peeled and grated
1 tablespoon **olive oil**
salt and **black pepper**

Mix all the ingredients for the pesto together in a small serving bowl and season with a little salt and plenty of black pepper. Set aside.

Heat the oil in a large, heavy saucepan, add the onion and butternut squash, and cook over medium-high heat for 5–6 minutes, until softened and golden in places. Add the coconut milk, curry paste, and stock and bring to a boil, stirring constantly. Cover and simmer gently for 30 minutes, until the squash is tender.

Transfer the soup, in batches, to a blender or food processor and blend until smooth. Return to the pan and reheat. Ladle into warm serving bowls, spoon a little of the pesto over the soup, and swirl through with a knife.

For spiced squash soup with extra-hot red chile pesto, mix together 1 finely chopped red chile, ¼ cup chopped cilantro, 1 tablespoon olive oil, and ½ teaspoon coarsely chopped cumin seeds for the pesto. Heat 3 tablespoons olive oil in a large saucepan, add 1 peeled, seeded, and chopped butternut squash (or 2 large prepared acorn squash), and 1 chopped onion, and cook over medium-high heat for 5–6 minutes, until softened and golden in places. Add ½ finely chopped red chile and 1 teaspoon each ground cumin and ground coriander and cook for another 2 minutes, stirring constantly. Add 3¾ cups vegetable stock and bring to a boil. Cover and simmer for 20 minutes, until the squash is tender. Season with salt and black pepper. Blend the soup, in batches, in a blender or food processor until smooth, then reheat. Ladle into warm serving bowls and top each with a spoonful of the pesto.

red bean soup cajun style

Serves **6**

Preparation time **25 minutes**, plus overnight soaking

Cooking time **1 hour**

2 tablespoons **sunflower oil**

1 large **onion**, chopped

1 **red bell pepper**, cored, seeded, and diced

1 **carrot**, peeled and diced

1 **baking potato**, peeled and diced

2–3 **garlic cloves**, chopped (optional)

2 teaspoons **Cajun spice mix**

1 (14½ oz) can **diced tomatoes**

1 tablespoon packed **dark brown sugar**

4 cups **vegetable stock**

1 (15 oz) can **red kidney beans**, drained

⅓ cup trimmed and sliced **okra**

½ cup trimmed and thinly sliced **green beans**

salt and **black pepper**

Heat the oil in a large skillet, add the onion, and cook over medium heat for 5 minutes, until softened. Add the red bell pepper, carrot, potato, and garlic, if using, and cook for another 5 minutes. Stir in the spice mix, tomatoes, sugar, stock, and plenty of salt and black pepper and bring to a boil.

Stir the kidney beans into the pan and bring to a boil, then cover and simmer for 45 minutes, until the vegetables are tender.

Add the green vegetables, replace the lid, and simmer for 5 minutes, until just cooked. Serve with crusty bread.

For Hungarian paprika & red bean soup, make the soup as above, using 1 teaspoon paprika instead of the Cajun spice mix. Simmer for 45 minutes. Omitting the green vegetables, transfer the soup, in batches, to a blender or food processor and blend until smooth, then reheat. Ladle into warm serving bowls and serve topped with 2 tablespoons plain soy yogurt sprinkled with a few caraway seeds.

chile miso soup

Serves **4**
Preparation time **20 minutes**
Cooking time **10 minutes**

2 tablespoons **miso paste**
1 tablespoon **dark soy sauce**
6 cups **vegetable stock**
5 oz **dried thin rice noodles**
1 inch piece of **fresh ginger
   root**, peeled and grated
1 tablespoon **sesame oil**
½ **red Thai chile**, seeded
   and finely chopped
3 cups diagonally sliced
   sugar snap peas
2 **shallots**, finely chopped
8 **baby corn**, coarsely sliced
⅓ cup chopped **cilantro**
2 **scallions**, finely sliced,
   to garnish

Put the miso paste, soy sauce, and stock into a large saucepan and bring to a boil. Reduce the heat, add the noodles and ginger, and simmer for 5 minutes.

Meanwhile, heat the oil in a wok or large skillet, add the chile, sugar snap peas, shallots, and baby corn, and stir-fry over medium-high heat for 5 minutes until softened.

Transfer the vegetable mixture to the pan with the stock and noodles, add the cilantro, and stir through. Serve in warm serving bowls, garnished with scallions.

For miso soup with ramen peppers & tofu, prepare the miso stock as above, then add 6 oz dried ramen noodles in place of the thin rice noodles and simmer for 5 minutes. Heat 1 tablespoon sesame oil in a wok or large skillet, add 1 red and 1 yellow bell peppers, cored, seeded, and thinly sliced, with 1 cup coarsely chopped sugar snap peas, and stir-fry over medium-high heat for 5 minutes, until softened. Add 4 oz firm tofu, drained, patted dry, and cubed, and gently toss for a few seconds, then transfer the mixture to the pan with the stock and noodles. Stir through, then serve ladled into warm bowls.

chickpea minestrone with arugula

Serves **4**
Preparation time **20 minutes**
Cooking time **30 minutes**

2 tablespoons **olive oil**
1 **red onion**, finely chopped
1 **garlic clove**, sliced
1 (15 oz) can **chickpeas**,
   drained and rinsed
1½ cups trimmed and
   diagonally sliced
   green beans
12 **cherry tomatoes**
3¾ cups **vegetable stock**
1¼ cups **tomato juice**
5 oz **dried whole-wheat
   pasta shapes**
2¾ cups **arugula leaves**
⅓ cup chopped **flat leaf
   parsley**
salt and **black pepper**

Heat the oil in a large, deep saucepan, add the onion, and cook over medium-high heat for 3–4 minutes, until beginning to soften. Add the garlic and cook, stirring, for 1 minute.

Add the chickpeas, green beans, and tomatoes to the pan and stir well, then stir in the stock, tomato juice, and pasta. Bring to a boil, then cover and simmer for 15 minutes, until the pasta is tender.

Remove the lid and continue to cook for another 10 minutes, adding three-quarters of the arugula and the parsley just before the end of cooking and stirring through. Season generously with salt and black pepper.

Serve in warm serving bowls with the remaining arugula sprinkled over to garnish, along with warm crusty whole-wheat bread.

For a chile, tomato & cannellini bean soup, heat 2 tablespoons olive oil in a saucepan, add 1 finely chopped red onion, and cook over medium heat for 5 minutes. Add ½ small red chile, finely chopped, and cook for 1 minute. Stir in 16 cherry tomatoes, then add 2½ cups vegetable stock, 1¼ cups tomato juice, and 1 (15 oz) can cannellini beans, drained and rinsed, and bring to a boil. Cover and simmer for 20 minutes, then add 4 cups coarsely chopped spinach leaves and stir through until wilted. Season with salt and black pepper, then serve in warm serving bowls with chunks of crusty bread.

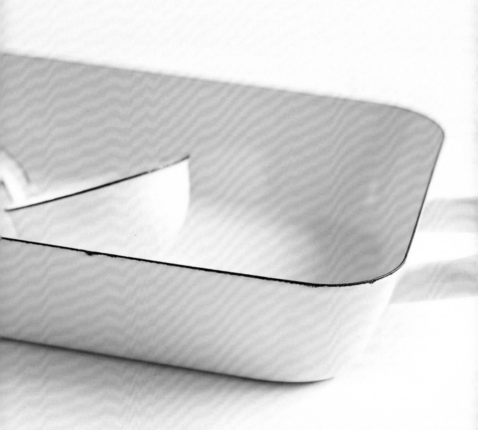

main dishes

provençale tart

Serves **6**

Preparation time **20 minutes**, plus proving

Cooking time **1 hour**

1²⁄₃ cups **white bread flour**, plus extra for dusting

1 teaspoon **salt**

1 teaspoon **sugar**

1 teaspoon **active dry yeast**

1 tablespoon **olive oil**

¹⁄₃ cup **lukewarm water**

Topping

¼ cup **olive oil**

4–5 **onions** (about 2 lb), sliced

1 **garlic clove**, crushed

1 teaspoon **thyme leaves**, plus extra to garnish

1 teaspoon **dried mixed herbs**

12 **pitted black ripe olives**

12 **cherry tomatoes**, halved

2 tablespoons **capers**

salt and **black pepper**

Mix together the flour, salt, sugar, and yeast in a bowl. Add the oil and measured lukewarm water and mix with your hand until the mixture comes together into a dough and leaves the sides of the bowl clean. If too dry, add a little more lukewarm water.

Turn out the dough onto a lightly floured surface and knead for about 10 minutes, until smooth and stretchy. Put in a clean bowl, cover with plastic wrap, and let rise in a warm place for about 1 hour, until doubled in size.

Meanwhile, make the topping. Heat the oil in a large skillet, add the onions, garlic, thyme, and dried herbs and cook, covered, over gentle heat, stirring occasionally, for about 30 minutes, until the onions are meltingly soft.

Turn out the dough onto a lightly floured surface and knead for 1 minute. Roll out the dough and use to line a 13 x 9 inch jellyroll pan. Spread the cooked onions over the top, sprinkle with the olives, tomatoes, and capers and season with salt and black pepper. Bake in a preheated oven, at 350°F, for 25 minutes, until golden. Garnish with thyme leaves and serve warm or cold.

For tomato tart with basil oil, make the dough and use to line a jellyroll pan as above. Sprinkle 2 thinly sliced garlic cloves over the dough, then top with 6 thinly sliced tomatoes. Blend a small handful of basil leaves with 3 tablespoons olive oil in a blender and drizzle over the tomatoes. Season with salt and black pepper and bake as above. Serve warm.

teriyaki mushrooms & noodles

Serves **4**
Preparation time **10 minutes**
Cooking time **10 minutes**

1 tablespoon **canola oil**
12 oz **assorted mushrooms,
such as shitake, open cup,**
and **oyster**, trimmed and
halved if large
¼ cup **mirin** or **dry sherry**
¼ cup **soy sauce**
1 tablespoon packed **light
brown sugar**
¾ inch piece of **fresh ginger
root**, peeled and grated
1 teaspoon **sesame oil**
10 oz **dried wide rice
noodles**
3 cups **sugar snap peas**
½ cup **sweet chili sauce**

Heat the canola oil in a wok or large skillet, add the
mushrooms, and stir-fry over high heat for 3 minutes,
until browned and tender.

Mix together the mirin or sherry, soy sauce, sugar,
ginger, and sesame oil in a small bowl and add to
the pan. Cook, stirring occasionally, for 3–4 minutes,
until the sauce has reduced slightly and coats the
mushrooms.

Meanwhile, cook the rice noodles and sugar snap peas
in a saucepan of boiling water for 2 minutes, or until the
noodles are tender and the sugar snap peas still have
a crunch to them. Drain and return to the pan, then add
the sweet chili sauce and toss to lightly coat.

Divide the noodles and sugar snap peas among
4 bowls and spoon the mushrooms and sauce over
the top.

For teriyaki tofu with cashew nuts, mix ¼ cup each
mirin or dry sherry and soy sauce with 1 tablespoon
packed light brown sugar, ¾ inch piece of fresh ginger
root, peeled and grated, and 1 teaspoon sesame oil in
a bowl. Add 11½ oz firm tofu, drained, patted dry, and
cubed, and turn to coat in the sauce, then let marinate
for 5 minutes. Heat 1 tablespoon canola oil in a wok or
large skillet, add the tofu, removing from the marinade
with a slotted spoon, and stir-fry over high heat for
1 minute, trying not to break up the tofu too much. Pour
in the remaining marinade and cook for another minute.
Serve with rice noodles sprinkled with 1 finely chopped
red chile and ½ cup chopped toasted cashew nuts.

saffron-scented vegetable stew

Serves **4**
Preparation time **15 minutes**
Cooking time **50 minutes**

½ cup **sunflower oil**
1 large **onion**, finely chopped
2 **garlic cloves**, finely chopped
2 teaspoons **ground coriander**
2 teaspoons **ground cumin**
2 teaspoons **ground cinnamon**
1 (15 oz) can **chickpeas**, drained
1 (14½ oz) can **diced tomatoes**
2½ cups **vegetable stock**
¼ teaspoon **saffron threads**
1 large **eggplant**, trimmed and chopped
4 cups trimmed **button mushrooms**, halved if large
½ cup chopped **dried figs**
2 tablespoons chopped **fresh cilantro**
salt and **black pepper**

Heat 2 tablespoons of the oil in a skillet, add the onion, garlic, and spices, and cook over medium heat, stirring frequently, for about 5 minutes, until the onion is golden.

Transfer the onion mixture to a saucepan with a slotted spoon and add the chickpeas, tomatoes, stock, and saffron. Season with salt and black pepper.

Heat the remaining oil in the skillet, add the eggplant, and cook over high heat, stirring frequently, for about 5 minutes, until browned. Add to the chickpea mixture and bring to a boil, then cover and simmer gently for 20 minutes.

Stir in the mushrooms and figs and simmer gently, uncovered, for another 20 minutes. Stir in the chopped cilantro and season with salt and black pepper. Serve with steamed whole-wheat couscous.

For winter vegetable & lentil stew, cook the onion, garlic, and spices as above, then transfer to a saucepan and add 1 drained (15 oz) can green lentils in place of the chickpeas, along with the tomatoes, stock, and saffron. Instead of the eggplant, cook 2 peeled and sliced carrots and 2 peeled and cubed potatoes in the remaining oil, then add to the lentil mixture. Continue as above, replacing the figs with ⅔ cup chopped dried apricots.

thai chickpea burgers

Serves **4**
Preparation time **20 minutes**
Cooking time **10 minutes**

4 **scallions**
1 stalk l**emon grass**, outer
leaves removed
¾ inch piece of **fresh ginger**,
peeled and chopped
1 **red chile**, halved and
seeded
1 **garlic clove**, peeled
handful of **cilantro leaves**
1 (15 oz) can **chickpeas**,
drained
2 tablespoons **whole-wheat
flour**
3 tablespoons **canola oil**
salt and **black pepper**

Pulse together the scallions, lemon grass, ginger, chile, garlic, and cilantro leaves in a food processor until finely chopped. Add the chickpeas and then pulse again until coarsely blended.

Add the flour and season with salt and black pepper, then process until the mixture forms a coarse thick paste. Shape the mixture into 4 patties.

Heat the oil in a skillet, add the burgers, and cook for 2–3 minutes on each side, until browned. Serve with a bean sprout and bell pepper salad, if desired.

For Mexican bean burgers, pulse together 4 scallions, 1 garlic clove, a handful of cilantro leaves, and 1 teaspoon each chili powder, ground cumin, and ground coriander in a food processor. Add 2 drained, canned mixed beans, such as kidney beans, cannellini beans, and chickpeas, and pulse again until coarsely blended. Add 2 tablespoons whole-wheat flour and 3 tablespoons plain soy yogurt and season with salt and black pepper. Blend until the mixture forms a coarse thick paste. Shape into 4 patties and cook as above. Serve in buns with guacamole and tomato salsa.

garlicky bean & mixed veg roast

Serves **4**
Preparation time **15 minutes**
Cooking time **40 minutes**

1 **green bell pepper**, cored,
    seeded, and cut into chunks
1 **red bell pepper**, cored,
    seeded, and cut into chunks
1 **yellow bell pepper**, cored,
    seeded, and cut into chunks
1 **eggplant**, trimmed and
    cut into chunks
1 **zucchini**, trimmed and sliced
1 **red onion**, cut into wedges
a few **rosemary sprigs**
a few **thyme sprigs**
¼ cup **olive oil**
4 **tomatoes**, cut into wedges
2 cups trimmed **button
    mushrooms**
4 **garlic cloves**, unpeeled
1 (15 oz) can **great Northern
    beans**, drained
2 tablespoons **balsamic
    vinegar**
½ cup **black ripe olives**
salt and **black pepper**

Put the bell peppers, eggplant, zucchini, onion, rosemary, and thyme in a large roasting pan. Drizzle with the oil, season with salt and black pepper, and toss until evenly coated in the oil, then spread out in a single layer. Roast a preheated oven, at 400°F, for 20 minutes, until starting to soften.

Add the tomatoes, mushrooms, and garlic cloves and mix with the other vegetables, then roast for another 10 minutes, until all the vegetables are tender.

Squeeze the soft garlic out of its skin onto the vegetables in the pan. Add the beans and vinegar and mix well. Return to the oven for a final 10 minutes. Sprinkle with the olives and serve with crusty bread.

For roasted vegetable tart, put 3 red, green, yellow, or orange bell peppers, cored, seeded, and cut into chunks, in a roasting pan with 1 onion, cut into wedges, and 1 sliced zucchini. Drizzle with 3 tablespoons olive oil, season with salt and black pepper, and toss until evenly coated in the oil, then spread out in a single layer. Roast in a preheated, at 400°F, for 20 minutes, until tender and lightly charred. Add 3 tomatoes, cut into wedges, sprinkle with 2 chopped garlic cloves and 1 tablespoon each chopped rosemary and thyme. Drizzle with 2 tablespoons balsamic vinegar and toss all the ingredients together. Unroll a sheet of ready-to-use vegan puff pastry, thawed if frozen, onto a baking sheet. Spread the vegetables over the pastry, leaving a border around the edge, and bake in the oven for 20–25 minutes, until the pastry is crisp and golden.

bok choy with chile & ginger

Serves **4**

Preparation time **5 minutes**

Cooking time **5 minutes**

1 tablespoon **peanut oil**

½ **chile**, sliced into rings

1 tablespoon peeled and
chopped **fresh ginger root**

large pinch of **salt**

½ large head of **bok choy**,
leaves separated

½ cup **water**

¼ teaspoon **sesame oil**

Heat the peanut oil in a wok or large skillet over high heat until the oil starts to shimmer. Add the chile, ginger, and salt and stir-fry for 15 seconds.

Add the bok choy to the pan and stir-fry for 1 minute, then add the measured water and continue cooking and stirring until the bok choy is tender and the water has evaporated.

Add the sesame oil to the pan, toss well, and serve immediately.

herbed quinoa stuffed tomatoes

Serves **4**

Preparation time **20 minutes**

Cooking time **40–50 minutes**

⅓ cup **quinoa**, rinsed and drained

4 large **beefsteak tomatoes**

½ small **red onion**, finely chopped

½ cup drained and sliced **roasted peppers** from a jar

1 **red chile**, seeded and chopped

2 tablespoons chopped **flat leaf parsley**

2 tablespoon chopped **cilantro**

2 tablespoons **sunflower seeds**

1 teaspoon **sesame oil**

1 tablespoon **soy sauce**, plus extra to serve

2 tablespoons **olive oil**

black pepper

Add the quinoa to a saucepan of boiling water, then simmer for 10–12 minutes, until tender. Drain, rinse in cold water, and drain again.

Meanwhile, cut the tops off the tomatoes and hollow out the centers with a teaspoon. Put half the tomato pulp and seeds in a bowl, discarding the rest, add the onion, roasted peppers, chile, parsley, cilantro, and sunflower seeds, and mix well.

Stir the sesame oil and soy sauce together and pour into the bowl. Mix well, then add the quinoa and mix again. Season with black pepper; the soy sauce is salty, so you won't need to add extra salt.

Sit the tomato shells on a baking sheet. Spoon the quinoa mixture into the tomatoes, drizzle with the olive oil, and bake a preheated oven, at 375°F, for 30–35 minutes, until the tomatoes are tender.

For slow-roasted tomato quinoa salad, cook the quinoa, then rinse and drain as above. Cut 6 tomatoes in half and put in a roasting pan with 1 thinly sliced garlic clove and a few thyme and rosemary sprigs. Drizzle with 2 tablespoons olive oil, season with salt and black pepper, and bake in a preheated oven, at 325°F, for about 1½ hours, until soft. Mix the tomatoes and their juices from the pan with the cooked quinoa, 1 small red onion, thinly sliced, 1 finely chopped red chile, and 2 tablespoons each sunflower seeds and chopped flat leaf parsley. Mix 1 tablespoon soy sauce and 1 teaspoon sesame oil together, pour it over the salad, and toss to mix. Serve with arugula or watercress.

gnocchi in tomato & leek sauce

Serves 4

Preparation time **30 minutes**

Cooking time **25 minutes**

5 **russet potatoes**, scrubbed
1 cup **all-purpose flour**
salt and **black pepper**

Sauce

1 tablespoon **olive oil**
1 **leek**, trimmed, cleaned,
   and chopped
1 **garlic clove**, crushed
4 **ripe tomatoes**, coarsely
   chopped
1 tablespoon **tomato paste**
pinch of **sugar**
small handful of torn **basil**
   leaves
salt and **black pepper**

Cook the potatoes in their skins in a saucepan of salted boiling water for about 20 minutes, until tender. Drain and let stand until cool enough to handle but not cold.

Meanwhile, make the sauce. Heat the oil in a skillet, add the leek, and cook over medium heat for 5 minutes, until tender. Add the garlic and tomatoes and cook for 5 minutes, until soft. Stir in the tomato paste and a little water to make a sauce. Add the sugar, season with salt and black pepper, and simmer for 3 minutes.

Peel off the potato skins and pass the potatoes through a potato ricer or mash with a potato masher until smooth. Season with salt and black pepper and knead in the flour to form a dough. Divide the gnocchi dough into 4 pieces and roll each into a thick log. Cut into ¾ inch pieces and press with the prongs of a fork to mark a ridged pattern.

Cook the gnocchi in a large saucepan of salted boiling water for 1–2 minutes, until they float to the surface. Remove from the pan with a slotted spoon and add to the sauce. Add the basil and gently turn the gnocchi to coat in the sauce. Serve with extra black pepper.

For fried gnocchi with broccoli & lemon, make the gnocchi as above (or use store-bought vegan gnocchi). Cook 3 cups broccoli florets in a saucepan of boiling salted water for 3 minutes, until just tender, then drain. Meanwhile, heat 3 tablespoons olive oil in a large skillet, add the gnocchi, and sauté for 8–10 minutes, until golden and crisp. Stir in 1 chopped red chile, 1 crushed garlic clove, the finely grated zest of 1 lemon, and the broccoli and heat through for 3 minutes.

roasted stuffed peppers

Serves **2**
Preparation time **10 minutes**
Cooking time **1 hour**

4 large **red bell peppers**
2 **garlic cloves**, crushed
1 tablespoon **chopped thyme**,
  plus extra to garnish
4 **plum tomatoes**, halved
¼ cup **extra virgin olive oil**
2 tablespoons **balsamic
  vinegar**
salt and **black pepper**

Cut the red bell peppers in half lengthwise, then scoop out and discard the cores and seeds. Put the pepper halves, cut side up, in a roasting pan lined with aluminum foil or in a ceramic dish. Divide the garlic and thyme among them and season with salt and black pepper.

Put a tomato half in each bell pepper and drizzle with the oil and vinegar. Roast in a preheated oven, at 425°F, for 55 minutes–1 hour, until the bell peppers are soft and charred.

Serve with some crusty bread to mop up the juices and a leafy green salad, if desired.

For roasted stuffed mushrooms, place 4 large portobello mushrooms, trimmed, gill side up on a baking sheet and lightly brush with 1 tablespoon olive oil. Roast in a preheated oven, at 425°F, for 10 minutes. Meanwhile, coarsely chop 1 large plum tomato and toss in a small bowl with 1 thinly sliced garlic clove, 1 tablespoon chopped thyme leaves, 1 teaspoon balsamic vinegar, and plenty of salt and black pepper. Remove from the oven and spoon the tomato filling into the mushrooms, slightly piling it around the stems. Return to the oven for another 10 minutes, until the filling is softened. Serve on warm serving plates with the juices spooned alongside together with warm crusty bread to mop up the juices.

cauliflower & butternut balti

Serves **4**
Preparation time **15 minutes**
Cooking time **20 minutes**

1 tablespoon **sunflower oil**
1 **onion**, chopped
1 **red bell pepper**, cored,
    seeded, and cut into chunks
1 teaspoon **mustard seeds**
1 teaspoon **fennel seeds**
2 **garlic cloves**, crushed
¾ inch piece of **fresh ginger
    root**, peeled and grated
2 teaspoons **garam masala**
2 teaspoons **ground cumin**
1 teaspoon **ground coriander**
1 teaspoon **ground turmeric**
½ teaspoon **dried red
    pepper flakes**
½ **butternut squash**, peeled,
    seeded, and cut into chunks
1 **cauliflower**, cut into florets
1 (14½ oz) can **diced
    tomatoes**
1¼ cups **water**
1⅓ cups **frozen peas**
1 cup **cashew nuts**, toasted
salt and **black pepper**

Heat the oil in a large saucepan, add the onion and red bell pepper, and cook over medium heat for 3 minutes, until softened. Add the mustard and fennel seeds and cook for 30 seconds, until starting to pop and smell fragrant. Add the garlic, ginger, garam masala, cumin, coriander, turmeric, and red pepper flakes and cook, stirring, for 30 seconds.

Add the butternut squash and cauliflower and stir to coat in the spices. Stir in the tomatoes and measured water, season with salt and black pepper, and bring to a boil, then cover and simmer for 10 minutes, stirring occasionally, until the vegetables are tender. Add the peas and cook for another 3 minutes.

Stir in half the cashew nuts and sprinkle the rest on the top to garnish. Serve with naan.

For cauliflower, coconut & spinach curry, heat 3 tablespoons sunflower oil in a large saucepan, add 1 chopped onion and 1 chopped red chile, and cook over medium heat for 3 minutes, until softened. Add 3 tablespoons vegan curry paste and cook, stirring, for 30 seconds. Add 1 cauliflower, cut into florets, and 8 oz new potatoes, scrubbed, and turn to coat in the spices. Stir in 1 (14½ oz) can diced tomatoes and 1 cup coconut milk, season with salt and black pepper, and bring to a boil, then cover and simmer for 10 minutes, until the cauliflower and potatoes are just cooked. Add 1⅓ cups frozen peas and cook for 3 minutes, then stir in 8 cups spinach leaves until just wilted. Sprinkle with toasted slivered almonds to serve.

nut roast packages

Serves **4**

Preparation time **30 minutes**

Cooking time **30 minutes**

3 tablespoons **canola oil**

1 **onion**, finely chopped

½ **red bell pepper**, cored, seeded, and finely chopped

1 **celery stick**, finely chopped

1 **carrot**, peeled and coarsely grated

1 cup trimmed and finely chopped **cremini mushrooms**

1 teaspoon **yeast extract**

1 cup **fresh white bread crumbs**

¾ cup **mixed nuts**, such as pistachio, blanched almonds, and cooked chestnuts, finely chopped

2 tablespoons **pine nuts**

2 tablespoons chopped **flat leaf parsley**

1 tablespoon chopped **rosemary**

1 tablespoon **whole-wheat flour**

8 sheets of **phyllo pastry**

green beans and roasted **cherry tomatoes**, to serve

Heat 1 tablespoon of the oil in a skillet, add the onion, red bell pepper, and celery and cook over gentle heat for 5 minutes, until softened. Add the carrot and mushrooms and cook for 5 minutes, until all the vegetables are tender.

Remove the pan from the heat and stir in the yeast extract, bread crumbs, nuts, pine nuts, parsley, rosemary, and flour. Season with salt and black pepper and mix together.

Brush one sheet of phyllo pastry with some of the remaining oil, then place a second on top. Spoon one-quarter of the nut mixture onto one end of the phyllo pastry and roll up, tucking in the ends as you roll to encase the filling. Put on a baking sheet. Repeat with the remaining pastry and filling to make 4 rolls. Brush the tops with oil.

Bake the packages in a preheated oven, at 375°F, for 20 minutes, until golden and crisp. Serve with green beans and roasted cherry tomatoes.

For nut roast meatballs, heat 1 tablespoon oil in a skillet, add 1 finely chopped onion, 1 finely chopped celery stick, and 1 crushed garlic clove, and cook over gentle heat for 5 minutes, until softened. Add 1 peeled and shredded carrot, ½ shredded zucchini, and 2 cups finely chopped mushrooms and cook for 5 minutes, until tender. Remove from the heat and stir in the yeast extract, bread crumbs, mixed nuts (omitting the pine nuts), herbs, flour, and salt and black pepper as above. Roll into 20 balls, place on a baking sheet, and bake in a preheated oven, at 400°F, for 15 minutes, until golden. Serve with spaghetti tossed in a jar of vegan tomato pasta sauce.

mixed vegetable chop suey

Serves **4**
Preparation time **10 minutes**
Cooking time **8 minutes**

1 tablespoon **cornstarch**
1 tablespoon **light soy sauce**
1 tablespoon **rice wine** or
  dry sherry
3 tablespoons **vegetable
  stock** or **water**
½ teaspoon **agave syrup**
2 tablespoons **peanut oil**
2 **red bell peppers**, cored,
  seeded, and cut into strips
2 **shallots**, finely sliced
1 teaspoon peeled and
  chopped **fresh ginger root**
2 **garlic cloves**, chopped
5 oz **shiitake mushrooms**,
  trimmed and halved
⅓ cup drained, canned
  sliced bamboo shoots
½ cup drained, canned
  sliced water chestnuts
3 cups **bean sprouts**
3 **scallions**, cut into
  1 inch lengths

Put the cornstarch in a small bowl with the soy sauce and rice wine or sherry and mix to a smooth paste. Stir in the stock or measured water and agave syrup and set the sauce aside.

Heat the oil in a wok or large skillet over high heat until the oil starts to shimmer. Add the red bell peppers, shallots, ginger, and garlic and stir-fry for 2 minutes, then add the mushrooms, bamboo shoots, and water chestnuts and stir-fry for another 2 minutes.

Add the bean sprouts to the pan with the scallions and the prepared sauce. Continue cooking for 1–2 minutes, or until the vegetables are coated in a rich velvety glaze. Serve immediately.

For red pepper & mushroom chop suey-style noodles, make the sauce as above and set aside. Heat the oil in a wok or large skillet as above, add 1 red bell pepper, cored, seeded, and cut into strips, 4 cups trimmed and quartered cremini mushrooms, and 2 finely sliced shallots and stir-fry for 3–4 minutes, until softened and golden. Add 1 teaspoon peeled and chopped fresh ginger root and 6 finely chopped scallions and stir-fry for 1 minute. Meanwhile, cook 6 oz dried rice noodles according to the package directions, then drain and set aside. Add the noodles to the pan along with the sauce and gently toss together for 2 minutes, until piping hot. Serve in deep warmed serving bowls with chopsticks.

basil & pine nut risotto

Serves **4**

Preparation time **20 minutes**

Cooking time **25 minutes**

3 cups **baby plum tomatoes**

3 tablespoons **olive oil**

2 **red onions**, thinly sliced

1 **garlic clove**, thinly sliced

¼ cup **pine nuts**

1 cup **risotto rice**

⅔ cup **white wine**

about 2½ cups **vegetable stock**, plus extra if needed

⅓ cup chopped **basil leaves**

salt and **black pepper**

vegan hard Parmesan-style cheese, finely grated, to serve

Put the tomatoes in a roasting pan and toss with 1 tablespoon of the oil until evenly coated, then spread out in a single layer. Roast in a preheated oven, at 400°F, for 20 minutes, until soft and lightly charred in places.

Meanwhile, heat the remaining oil in a large, heavy skillet, add the onions and garlic, and cook over medium-high heat for 5 minutes, until softened and beginning to turn golden.

Toast the pine nuts in a dry skillet over medium heat, shaking the pan occasionally, for 2–3 minutes, until golden. Set aside.

Add the rice to the onions and garlic and stir well to coat. Pour in the wine and half the stock and bring to a boil, then simmer gently, stirring, until the liquid is almost all absorbed. Stir in the remaining stock, then simmer gently, stirring frequently, for another 10–12 minutes, until it is almost all absorbed and the rice is tender and cooked through, adding more stock, if necessary. Add the basil and cook for 2–3 minutes, until wilted, then mix in the pine nuts.

Stir half the roasted tomatoes through the risotto and season well with salt and black pepper. Serve in warm serving bowls topped with the remaining tomatoes.

caper, lemon & chile spaghetti

Serves **4**

Preparation time **5 minutes**

Cooking time **12 minutes**

12 oz **spelt spaghetti**

1 (8 oz) package **baby broccoli,** cut into chunks

2 tablespoons **olive oil**

1 small **red onion,** finely sliced

1 **red chile,** seeded and chopped

2 tablespoons **capers**

finely grated zest of 1 **lemon** and 1 tablespoon juice

2 tablespoons **balsamic vinegar**

salt and **black pepper**

Cook the spaghetti in a large saucepan of salted boiling water for 10 minutes, adding the baby broccoli for the final 3 minutes, or until just tender.

Meanwhile, heat the oil in a skillet, add the onion and chile, and cook over gentle heat for 2 minutes. Stir in the capers, lemon zest and juice, and vinegar, season with salt and black pepper, and heat through.

Drain the spaghetti and broccoli, reserving 1 tablespoon of the cooking water and adding to the caper mixture. Add the drained spaghetti and broccoli to the pan and toss well to combine over the heat. Serve with an extra grinding of black pepper.

For artichoke, lemon & mint spaghetti, cook 12 oz of spaghetti as above, adding 1 cup frozen peas for the final 3 minutes, until just tender. Meanwhile, heat 2 tablespoons olive oil in a skillet, add two-thirds of 1 drained (14 oz) jar marinated artichokes in oil, and heat through for 1 minute. Stir in the finely grated zest of 1 lemon, 1 tablespoon lemon juice, and 2 tablespoons each balsamic vinegar and chopped mint and season with salt and black pepper. Drain the spaghetti and peas, reserving 1 tablespoon of the cooking water and adding to the artichoke mixture. Add the drained spaghetti and peas to the pan and toss well to combine over the heat. Serve with an extra grinding of black pepper.

veggie kebabs with bulgur wheat

Serves **4**
Preparation time **20 minutes**
Cooking time **20–25 minutes**

1 **red bell pepper**, cored,
   seeded, and cut into chunks
1 **yellow bell pepper**, cored,
   seeded, and cut into chunks
2 small **zucchini**, trimmed and
   thickly sliced
1 small **eggplant**, trimmed and
   cut into chunks
1 small **red onion**, quartered
8 **cremini mushrooms**,
   trimmed and halved
2 teaspoons **dried rosemary**
1 teaspoon **fennel seeds**
finely grated zest of 1 **lemon**
2 tablespoons **olive oil**
salt and **black pepper**

Bulgur wheat salad
3 cups **vegetable stock**
1¾ cups **bulgur wheat**
1 tablespoon **harissa**
½ cup **raisins**
2 **scallions**, finely sliced
2 tablespoons chopped **mint**
⅓ cup **sunflower seeds**

Put the vegetables in a bowl with the rosemary, fennel seeds, and lemon zest. Drizzle with the oil, season, and toss until the vegetables are evenly coated in the oil.

Thread the different vegetables alternately onto 4 long or 8 short metal skewers and cook under a preheated medium-hot broiler for 20–25 minutes, or until tender and browned, turning occasionally.

Meanwhile, bring the stock to a boil in a saucepan. Add the bulgur wheat, cover, and simmer for 7 minutes. Remove from the heat and let stand until the stock is absorbed.

Fork the harissa, raisins, scallions, mint, and sunflower seeds through the cooked bulgur wheat until combined, then spoon onto serving plates. Arrange the vegetable kebabs on the plates and serve immediately.

For roasted vegetables with harissa bulgur wheat, put 1 small red and 1 small yellow bell pepper, cored and cut into chunks, in a roasting pan with 2 small zucchini, thickly sliced, and 1 red onion, cut into wedges. Sprinkle with 2 tablespoons olive oil, 1 tablespoon chopped rosemary leaves, and 1 teaspoon fennel seeds and toss. Roast a preheated oven, at 400°F, for 25 minutes, until softened and charred in places. Meanwhile, add 1¾ cups bulgur wheat to 3 cups vegetable stock in a saucepan and bring to a boil, then simmer gently, stirring, for 7 minutes. Remove from the heat and let stand until the stock is absorbed. Add 1 tablespoon harissa and 2 tablespoons chopped mint, season with salt and black pepper, and fork together, then stir in the roasted vegetables.

potato, rosemary & onion pie

Serves **4**
Preparation time **30 minutes**
Cooking time **about 45
 minutes**

½ cup **olive oil**
1 large **Bermuda onion**,
 halved and thinly sliced
8 **red-skinned potatoes**
 (about 2 lb), scrubbed
 and thinly sliced
⅓ cup chopped **rosemary
 leaves**
½ teaspoon **dried red
 pepper flakes**
½ teaspoon **ground cumin**
½ teaspoon **ground coriander**
⅔ cup **vegetable stock**
1 (1 lb) package **ready-to-use
 vegan puff pastry**, thawed
 if frozen
all-purpose flour, for dusting
2 tablespoons **soy milk**
salt and **black pepper**

Heat half the oil in a skillet, add the onion, and cook over medium-high heat for 5 minutes, until softened and beginning to turn golden. Remove and set aside. Heat the remaining oil in the pan, add the potato slices, rosemary, and spices and cook, tossing and stirring frequently, for 10 minutes, until softened and lightly golden.

Layer the potato slices in a pie plate with the onions. Pour in the stock and season with salt and black pepper.

Roll the pastry out on a lightly floured surface to about ¾ inch wider than the top of the pie plate. Cut a thin strip of pastry and place around the edge of the dish, pressing down with a little water to seal. Lightly brush the top of the strip with water, top with the pastry lid, and press around the edges with a fork to seal. Make an incision in the center of the pie for the steam to escape and lightly brush all over with the soy milk.

Bake in a preheated oven, at 425°F, for 25–30 minutes, until the pastry is golden and the potatoes are tender. Serve hot.

For sweet potato & red onion pie with thyme, heat
¼ cup olive oil in a skillet, add 2 thinly sliced red onions, and cook over medium-high heat for 5 minutes, until softened. Remove and set aside. Heat another ¼ cup olive oil in the pan, add 6 sweet potatoes (about 2 lb), peeled and thinly sliced, and cook over medium heat, tossing and stirring frequently, for 10 minutes. Add 1 tablespoon ground coriander and ½ teaspoon dried red pepper flakes and cook for another minute. Follow the recipe above to layer in a pie plate with the onions, add the stock, top the pie with pastry, and bake.

pea & mint pesto fettuccine

Serves **4**

Preparation time **20 minutes**

Cooking time **10–12 minutes**

8 oz **dried egg-free
    fettuccine**

1⅔ cups **frozen peas**, thawed

1 **garlic clove**, coarsely
    chopped

1 teaspoon **wasabi**

⅓ cup **mint leaves**

⅓ cup **olive oil**

2 tablespoons **pine nuts**

⅔ cup **water**

salt and **black pepper**

mint leaves, to garnish

crusty bread, to serve

Cook the fettuccine in a large saucepan of lightly salted boiling water for 8–10 minutes, or according to package directions, until just tender.

Meanwhile, blend together the peas, garlic, wasabi, mint, oil, pine nuts, and measured water in a blender or food processor until well combined. Season with plenty of salt and black pepper.

Drain the pasta well and return to the pan with the pea pesto. Toss over gentle heat for 2–3 minutes, until piping hot. Sprinkle with the mint leaves and serve immediately in warm serving bowls with crusty bread.

For basil pesto with fettuccine, cook 12 oz dried egg-free fettuccine as above. Meanwhile, blend together 1 whole garlic clove, 2 handfuls of basil leaves, ⅓ cup olive oil, and 3 tablespoons pine nuts in a blender or food processor until smooth. Season well with salt and black pepper. Drain the pasta well and return to the pan with the basil pesto. Toss over gentle heat for 1–2 minutes, until piping hot, then serve immediately in warm serving bowls.

sage & tomato pilaf

Preparation time **15 minutes**
Cooking time **40–45 minutes**
Serves **4**

8 **plum tomatoes**
1 **red bell pepper**, cored,
    seeded, and quartered
1 **onion**, coarsely chopped
2 tablespoons **olive oil**
small bunch of **sage**
1 cup **mixed instant white
    long-grain** and **wild rice**
salt and **black pepper**

Cut each tomato into 8 and thickly slice the bell pepper quarters. Place in a roasting pan with the onion, then drizzle with the oil and season well with salt and black pepper. Tear some of the sage into pieces and sprinkle them over the vegetables. Roast in a preheated oven, at 400°F, for 40–45 minutes, until the vegetables are softened.

Meanwhile, cook the rice in a saucepan of boiling water for 15 minutes, or until only just cooked.

Drain the cooked rice and mix into the roasted vegetables. Spoon into warm serving bowls and sprinkle with the remaining sage leaves. Serve with warm ciabatta or herb bread.

For sage & tomato rice with olives, heat 3 tablespoons olive oil in a large, heavy skillet, add 1 large onion, finely chopped, and 1 red bell pepper, cored, seeded, and coarsely chopped, and cook over medium-high heat for 3–4 minutes, until softened. Stir in ⅓ cup coarsely chopped sage and 1½ cups red rice, then add 2½ cups vegetable stock. Bring to a boil, then cover and simmer gently, stirring occasionally, for 20 minutes, or according to package directions, until the rice is tender and cooked through, adding a little more stock, if necessary. Meanwhile, heat 1 tablespoon olive oil in a separate skillet, add 16 cherry tomatoes, and cook gently for 3–4 minutes, until softened and the skins have burst. Stir into the rice once the rice is cooked, season with salt and black pepper, and serve.

cauliflower & chickpea pan-fry

Serves **4**
Preparation time **20 minutes**
Cooking time **20 minutes**

⅓ cup **olive oil**
1 **red onion**, cut into thin
  wedges
½ **cauliflower**, cut into small
  florets
1 teaspoon **garam masala**
1 teaspoon **ground coriander**
¼ cup **water**, plus ⅓ cup
28 **Swiss chard leaves**,
  washed, patted dry, and
  cut into strips
1 teaspoon **cumin seeds**
1 **garlic clove**, thinly sliced
1 (15 oz) can **chickpeas**,
  drained and rinsed
⅓ cup **tahini**
¼ cup **lemon juice**
salt and **black pepper**
naan or **pita bread**, to serve

Heat the oil in a large, heavy skillet or wok, add the
onion, and cook over medium-high heat, stirring
frequently, for 3–4 minutes, until beginning to soften.
Add the cauliflower florets, garam masala, and ground
coriander and cook for 5 minutes, stirring almost
constantly to prevent the cauliflower from catching,
then add the ¼ cup cold water and cook for another
2 minutes, stirring almost constantly.

Stir the chard leaves, cumin seeds, and garlic into
the pan and cook, stirring, for another 2 minutes.
Add the chickpeas along with the tahini, lemon
juice and remaining measured water and season
with salt and black pepper. Toss the vegetables in
the sauce, then reduce the heat, cover, and simmer
for 2 minutes. Season generously with salt and
black pepper.

Toss again before serving in warm serving bowls with
naan or pita bread.

For curried broccoli pan-fry with cumin seeds,
heat 3 tablespoons olive oil in a large, heavy skillet or
wok, add 1 large white onion, thinly sliced into wedges,
and stir-fry over medium-high heat for 2 minutes. Add
3 cups small broccoli florets and 1 red bell pepper, cored,
seeded, and thinly sliced, and stir-fry for 3–4 minutes,
until softened. Add 2 tablespoons curry paste and
1 teaspoon cumin seeds and cook, stirring, for another
1 minute. Add 2 tablespoons mango chutney, season
with salt and black pepper, if necessary, and toss again
for 1 minute. Serve piled onto 2 warm, halved naan or
pita breads.

ratatouille and parsnip casserole

Serves **6**

Preparation time **25 minutes**

Cooking time **45 minutes**

¹⁄₃ cup **olive oil**

1 **red bell pepper**, cored, seeded, and cut into chunks

1 **green bell pepper**, cored, seeded, and cut into chunks

1 **yellow bell pepper**, cored, seeded, and cut into chunks

1 **garlic clove**, thinly sliced

1 large **eggplant**, trimmed and cut into chunks

2 **zucchini**, trimmed and cut into chunks

5 **tomatoes**, coarsely chopped

²⁄₃ cup **red wine**

²⁄₃ cup **water**

1 **vegetable bouillon cube**

10 **parsnips** (about 2½ lb), peeled and chopped

2 tablespoons **soy spread**

1 tablespoon chopped **thyme leaves**

salt and **black pepper**

Heat the oil in a large, heavy skillet, add the bell peppers, garlic, eggplant, and zucchini, and cook over medium-high heat, stirring and tossing occasionally, for 10 minutes, until softened and lightly golden in places. Add the tomatoes and cook for 3 minutes. Pour in the wine and measured water and bring to a boil, then cover and simmer for another 10 minutes.

Meanwhile, bring a large saucepan of lightly salted water to a boil, crumble in the bouillon cube with the parsnips, and mix well. Bring to a gentle simmer and cook for 10 minutes, until the parsnips are tender. Drain well, return to the pan, and mash with the soy spread, then stir in the thyme leaves.

Transfer the ratatouille mixture to a large gratin dish. Spoon the mashed parsnips over the vegetables and season generously with black pepper. Bake in a preheated oven, at 400°F, for 20 minutes, until the top is lightly golden in places. Serve with a green salad.

For baked roasted vegetables with parsnips, seed and cut 3 red, green, yellow, or orange bell peppers into chunks, then put them into a large roasting pan with 2 zucchini, trimmed and cut into chunks, and 2 parsnips, peeled and cut into chunks. Drizzle with ¼ cup olive oil, sprinkle with 2 tablespoons chopped rosemary, and season with salt and black pepper. Roast in a preheated oven, at 400°F, for 20 minutes, until soft and lightly golden in places. Add 4 tomatoes, cut into chunks, to the pan and gently toss, then roast for another 10 minutes. Serve hot in warm serving bowls with crusty bread to mop up the juices.

squash, carrot & mango stew

Serves **4**

Preparation time **15 minutes**

Cooking time **35–40 minutes**

2 tablespoons **olive oil**

1 large **onion**, cut into large chunks

3 **garlic cloves**, finely chopped

1 **butternut squash**,peeled, seeded, and cubed

2 small **carrots**, peeled and cut into thick batons

½ inch **cinnamon stick**

½ teaspoon **ground turmeric**

¼ teaspoon **cayenne pepper** (optional)

½ teaspoon **ground cumin**

1 teaspoon **paprika**

pinch of **saffron threads**

1 tablespoon **tomato paste**

3 cups **hot vegetable stock**

1 **mango**, peeled, pitted, and cut into 1 inch chunks

salt and **black pepper**

2 tablespoons chopped **cilantro**, to garnish

Heat the oil in a large, heavy saucepan, add the onion, and cook over gentle heat for 5 minutes, until beginning to soften. Add the garlic, butternut squash, carrots, and spices and cook gently for 5 minutes.

Stir in the tomato paste, then pour in the stock and season with salt and black pepper. Cover and simmer gently for 20–25 minutes, until the vegetables are tender. Stir in the mango and simmer gently for another 5 minutes.

Ladle the stew into serving bowls, sprinkle with the cilantro to garnish, and serve with steamed couscous.

For spicy squash & carrot soup, make the stew as above, adding an extra 1 cup hot vegetable stock. Once the vegetables are tender, transfer to a blender or food processor and blend until smooth. Ladle into bowls and serve sprinkled with chopped cilantro and topped with a swirl of plain vegan yogurt.

eggplant & wheat berries salad

Serves **4**

Preparation time **20 minutes**,
plus standing and cooling

Cooking time about **5 minutes**

½ cup **olive oil**

1¼ cups **wheat berries**

1 teaspoon **ground coriander**

½ teaspoon **ground paprika**

½ teaspoon **chili powder**

1 cup **vegetable stock**

1 large **eggplant**, trimmed and
cut into ¾ inch cubes

1 cup **walnut pieces**

finely grated zest of 1 **lemon**

2 cups fresh **baby spinach
leaves**

handful of **cilantro leaves**

salt and **black pepper**

lemon wedges, to serve

Heat 1 tablespoon of the oil in a large, heavy saucepan, add the wheat berries and spices, and toss well to coat. Pour in the stock and bring to a boil, stirring constantly. Cover with a tight-fitting lid, remove from the heat, and let stand for 25 minutes, until all the liquid is absorbed and the grain is tender.

Meanwhile, heat the remaining oil in a heavy skillet, add the eggplant cubes, and cook over medium-high heat, turning occasionally, for 4–5 minutes, until golden all over and tender. Add the walnuts and toss over the heat for 1 minute.

Transfer the wheat berries to a large bowl and toss with the lemon zest, eggplant, and walnuts, then let cool for a few minutes before adding the spinach and cilantro leaves. Toss well and season with a little salt and plenty of black pepper, then serve with lemon wedges.

For zucchini & onion salad with barley couscous

& cilantro, heat 1 tablespoon olive oil in a saucepan, add 1¼ cups barley couscous, and ½ teaspoon each ground paprika and chili powder, and toss well to coat. Pour in 2 cups vegetable stock and bring to a boil, stirring constantly. Cover with a tight-fitting lid, remove from the heat, and let stand for 20 minutes. Meanwhile, heat ¼ cup olive oil in a large, heavy skillet, add 2 zucchini, trimmed and cubed, and cook over medium-heat, turning occasionally, for 4–5 minutes, until golden all over and tender. Toss into the swollen couscous along with 2 handfuls of cilantro leaves, the finely grated zest of 1 lemon, and a little salt and plenty of black pepper. Serve with lemon wedges.

pearl barley risotto with carrots

Serves **4**
Preparation time **15 minutes**,
  plus standing
Cooking time **25 minutes**

1 cup **pearl barley**
1 lb **baby carrots**, scrubbed
⅓ cup **olive oil**
1 large **onion**, finely chopped
1 large **leek**, trimmed, cleaned,
  and thinly sliced
1 **garlic clove**, thinly sliced
1 tablespoon **thyme leaves**
1 teaspoon **ground coriander**
5 cups **vegetable stock**, plus
  extra if needed
2 tablespoons chopped **flat
  leaf parsley**, to garnish
salt and **black pepper**
whole-wheat bread, to serve

Put the pearl barley in a bowl, pour over enough boiling water to cover, and let stand for 10 minutes.

Toss the carrots in a shallow roasting pan with 2 tablespoons of the oil until evenly coated, then roast in a preheated oven, at 400°F, for 20 minutes, until tender and lightly charred in places.

Meanwhile, heat the remaining oil in a skillet, add the onion and leek with the garlic and thyme, and cook over medium heat, stirring occasionally, for 4 minutes, until soft and pale golden. Stir in the ground coriander and cook for another 1 minute.

Drain the pearl barley, add to the skillet with half the stock, and bring to a boil. Cover and simmer gently, stirring occasionally, for about 10 minutes, until almost all the stock is absorbed. Add the remaining stock and stir, then cover and simmer gently again until the pearl barley is tender and some of the stock is still left in the pan, adding more stock, if necessary.

Add the roasted carrots to the risotto and stir through. Season and serve with warm whole-wheat bread.

For roasted root vegetable risotto, put 8 scrubbed baby carrots into a roasting pan with 2 parsnips, peeled and cut into batons, and 2 peeled and chopped turnips. Add 3 tablespoons olive oil and toss. Add 1 tablespoon chopped rosemary leaves and toss again. Roast in a preheated oven, at 400°F, for 20–25 minutes, until lightly charred and tender. Meanwhile, cook the onion, leek, and garlic as above, omitting the thyme, then add and cook the pearl barley as above. Fold in the roasted vegetables and season.

roasted peppers with quinoa

Serves **4**
Preparation time **15 minutes**,
 plus standing
Cooking time **45 minutes**

2 **Romano** or **long red sweet
 peppers**, halved, cored,
 and seeded
20 **yellow cherry tomatoes**,
 halved
2 large **yellow bell peppers**,
 halved, cored, and seeded
20 **red cherry tomatoes**,
 halved
1 teaspoon **cumin seeds**
2 tablespoons **olive oil**
1 ¼ cups **quinoa**
1 **onion**, finely chopped
½ teaspoon **ground ginger**
1 teaspoon **paprika**
pinch of freshly grated **nutmeg**
⅓ cup chopped **dried
 apricots**
⅓ cup **raisins**
⅓ cup chopped **pitted dried
 dates**
⅓ cup shelled **pistachio nuts**
¼ cup **slivered almonds**,
 toasted, plus extra to garnish
2 **scallions,** finely sliced
salt and **black pepper**

Fill the red sweet peppers with the yellow tomatoes and the yellow bell peppers with the red tomatoes. Put in a roasting pan, sprinkle with the cumin seeds, and drizzle with 1 tablespoon of the oil, then season well with salt and black pepper. Roast in a preheated oven, at 350°F, for about 45 minutes, or until tender and slightly blackened around the edges.

Meanwhile, rinse the quinoa several times in cold water. Drain, put into a saucepan, and cover with twice its volume of boiling water. Cover with a lid and simmer for about 12 minutes, or until the seed is coming away from the germ. Remove from the heat and let stand, covered, until all the water is absorbed.

Heat the remaining oil in a small skillet, add the onion, and cook over gentle heat for 10 minutes, until soft. Stir in the spices, dried fruits, and nuts and cook, stirring frequently, for another 3–4 minutes, or until the fruits have softened. Gently fold into the quinoa.

Pile the quinoa onto 4 plates and top each with 1 roasted red and 1 roasted yellow pepper half. Sprinkle with the scallions and extra slivered almonds and serve.

vegetable paella with almonds

Serves **4**

Preparation time **25 minutes**

Cooking time **30 minutes**

¼ cup **olive oil**

1 **onion**, chopped

pinch of **saffron threads**

1 ¼ cups **risotto rice**

5 cups **vegetable stock**

16 fine **asparagus spears**,
    trimmed and cut into
    2 inch lengths

bunch of **scallions**,
    cut into strips

12 **baby plum tomatoes**,
    halved

1 cup **frozen peas**

3 tablespoons **slivered
    almonds**, toasted

3 tablespoons chopped
    flat leaf parsley

salt

Heat 1 tablespoon of the oil in a large, heavy skillet, add the onion and saffron, and cook over medium heat, stirring frequently, for 5 minutes, until the onion is softened and golden. Add the rice and stir well, then season with some salt. Add the stock and bring to a boil, then cover and simmer, stirring occasionally, for 20 minutes, until the stock is almost all absorbed and the rice is tender and cooked through.

Meanwhile, heat the remaining oil in a separate skillet, add the asparagus and scallions, and cook over medium heat for 5 minutes, until softened and lightly charred in places. Remove from the pan with a slotted spoon. Add the tomatoes to the pan and cook for 2–3 minutes on each side, until softened.

Add the peas to the rice and cook for another 2 minutes, then add the asparagus, scallions, and tomatoes and gently toss through. Sprinkle with the almonds and parsley and serve.

For pepper & mushroom paella with pine nuts,

heat 2 tablespoons olive oil in a large, heavy skillet, add 1 red, 1 green, and 1 yellow bell pepper, cored, seeded, and thinly sliced, 3 cups quartered cremini mushrooms, and 1 small red onion, thinly sliced, and cook over medium heat for 4–5 minutes, until softened. Add 1 ¼ cups risotto rice and stir well, then season with some salt. Pour in 5 cups vegetable stock and bring to a boil, then cover and simmer for 20 minutes, until the stock is almost all absorbed and the rice is tender and cooked through. Remove from the heat and stir in 3 tablespoons each lightly toasted pine nuts and chopped flat leaf parsley.

mushroom stroganoff

Serves **4**
Preparation time **15 minutes**
Cooking time **10 minutes**

⅓ cup **olive oil**
1 lb **mixed mushrooms,**
    such as cremini, chanterelle,
    shiitake, and button,
    trimmed and halved or
    quartered if large
1 **garlic clove**, thinly sliced
1 large **red onion**, halved
    and thinly sliced
2 tablespoons **brandy**
1 teaspoon **whole-grain**
    mustard
½ teaspoon **English mustard**
½ teaspoon **ground paprika**
2 tablespoons **cashew butter**
1 cup **soy cream**
¼ cup chopped **flat leaf**
    parsley
salt and **black pepper**

Heat the oil in a large, heavy skillet, add the mushrooms, garlic, and onion, and cook over high heat, stirring occasionally, for 5 minutes, until golden and softened.

Add the brandy, mustards, and paprika and continue to cook, stirring and tossing constantly, for 1–2 minutes. Stir in the cashew butter and soy cream and gently heat for 1 minute, until piping hot but not boiling, otherwise the cream may separate.

Stir in the chopped parsley and season with a little salt and plenty of black pepper. Serve on a bed of rice.

For vegetable stroganoff, heat 3 tablespoons olive oil in a large, heavy skillet, add 1 large onion, thinly sliced, 2 sweet potatoes, peeled and cubed, and 1 red bell pepper, cored, seeded, and cubed, and cook over medium heat, stirring occasionally, for 5 minutes, until the onion is softened but not browned. Add ⅓ cup water and stir again. Cover and simmer gently for 5 minutes, or until the sweet potato is tender. Add ½ teaspoon ground paprika and toss again, then stir in 1 cup cashew cream and ¼ cup chopped flat leaf parsley and heat for 1–2 minutes over gentle heat until piping hot but not boiling, otherwise the cream may separate. Season well with salt and black pepper and serve on a bed of rice.

tindora & green mango curry

Serves **4**

Preparation time **20 minutes**

Cooking time **35 minutes**

⅔ cup **dried green lentils**, rinsed and drained

1 small **green mango**

1 small **red onion**, finely chopped

handful of chopped **cilantro**

3 tablespoons **vegetable oil**

1 teaspoon **ground turmeric**

2 teaspoons **garam masala**

1 teaspoon **cumin seeds**

1 teaspoon **black onion seeds**

1 **red chile**, finely chopped

1 **green chile,** finely chopped

3 large **tomatoes**, chopped

8 oz **tindora** (available online, also called **ivy gourd)**, rinsed, drained, and trimmed, or **baby zucchini**, thickly sliced

2 tablespoons packed **light brown sugar**

1 tablespoon **tamarind paste**

⅔ cup **boiling water**

salt and **black pepper**

chapatis, to serve

Cook the lentils in a saucepan of boiling water for 20 minutes, until soft. Drain well.

Meanwhile, peel and pit the mango, then shred the flesh finely and mix with the onion and cilantro. Cover and chill until required.

Heat the oil in a large saucepan, add the turmeric, garam masala, cumin seeds, and black onion seeds, and cook for 1–2 minutes, until the spices are sizzling and the mustard seeds begin to pop.

Stir the chiles, tomatoes, tindora (ivy gourd) or baby zucchini, and cooked lentils into the spice mixture, then cover and simmer gently, stirring occasionally, for 10 minutes. Mix the brown sugar and tamarind paste with the measured boiling water in a small bowl and add to the pan. Stir well and simmer for another 5 minutes. Season with salt and black pepper, then serve topped with the green mango and red onion mixture, along with chapatis.

turkish stuffed butternut squash

Serves **4**

Preparation time **25 minutes**

Cooking time **1 hour
5 minutes**

2 **butternut squashes**,
halved and seeded

¼ cup **olive oil**

salt and **black pepper**

Filling

3 tablespoons **olive oil**

1 large **onion**, finely chopped

1 **garlic clove**, thinly sliced

1 teaspoon **ground cumin**

4 **tomatoes**, coarsely chopped

¼ cup chopped **flat leaf
parsley**

1 tablespoon chopped
oregano

2 tablespoons **tomato paste**

1 teaspoon **cumin seeds**

salt and **black pepper**

Sit the squash halves, cut side up, in a large roasting pan, brush each with 1 tablespoon oil, and season with salt and black pepper. Roast in a preheated oven, at 425°F, for 45 minutes, until lightly charred on top.

Meanwhile, heat the oil for the filling in a large, heavy skillet, add the onion, garlic, and cumin, and cook over medium-high heat, stirring occasionally, for 4–5 minutes, until beginning to soften. Add the tomatoes, parsley, oregano, and tomato paste and cook, stirring occasionally, for another 5 minutes. Season well with salt and black pepper.

Divide the filling among the cavities of the roasted squash halves and sprinkle with the cumin seeds. Reduce the oven temperature to 350°F, and roast the stuffed squash for 20 minutes, or until the filling is soft and golden in places. Serve with a simple arugula salad, if desired.

For Turkish stuffed peppers with raisins, heat ¼ cup olive oil in a large skillet, add 2 coarsely chopped onions, 2 thinly sliced garlic cloves, and 2 teaspoons ground cumin, and cook over medium-high heat, stirring occasionally, for about 8 minutes, until the onions are soft. Stir in 6 coarsely chopped tomatoes, ⅓ cup raisins, ¼ cup chopped flat leaf parsley, and 2 tablespoons tomato paste, then cover and cook for another 5 minutes. Season with salt and black pepper. Fill 4 cored, seeded, and halved bell peppers with the mixture in a roasting pan, cover with aluminum foil, and bake in a preheated oven, at 350°F, for 20 minutes. Remove the foil and cook for another 10 minutes.

chunky tomato & bean stew

Serves **4**
Preparation time **15 minutes**
Cooking time **25 minutes**

2 tablespoons **olive oil**
1 **red onion**, chopped
1 **carrot**, peeled and cut
into chunks
2 **garlic cloves**, crushed
1 **zucchini**, trimmed and
cut into chunks
1 **red chile**, seeded and
chopped
2 teaspoons chopped
thyme leaves
2 teaspoons **smoked paprika**
1 (15 oz) can **mixed beans
in chili sauce**
1 (15 oz) can **chickpeas**,
drained
1 (14½ oz) can **diced
tomatoes**
⅔ cup **vegetable stock**
salt and **black pepper**
vegan tortilla chips, to serve

Heat the oil in a saucepan, add the onion and carrot, and cook over gentle heat for 5 minutes, until softened. Stir in the garlic, zucchini, chile, thyme, and smoked paprika and cook for another 5 minutes.

Stir the beans with their sauce, chickpeas, tomatoes, and stock into the pan. Bring to a boil, then simmer for 10 minutes, until the vegetables are tender and the stew has thickened slightly. Season with salt and black pepper and serve hot, with vegan tortilla chips.

For chunky tomato, bean & rice stew, heat 2 tablespoons olive oil in a saucepan, add 1 chopped onion, 1 cored, seeded, and chopped green bell pepper, 1 peeled and chopped carrot, 1 trimmed and chopped zucchini, 2 crushed garlic cloves, and 1 chopped red chile, and cook over medium heat for 5 minutes. Add 1 (15 oz) can mixed beans in chili sauce, 1 (14½ oz) can diced tomatoes, 1 cup vegetable stock, and 2 teaspoons each chopped thyme leaves and smoked paprika. Bring to a boil, then stir in 1 cup long-grain rice and simmer for 10–12 minutes, until the rice and vegetables are tender. Season with salt and black pepper and serve with a crisp green salad.

Asian-style risotto

Serves **4**
Preparation time **15 minutes**
Cooking time **25 minutes**

5 cups **vegetable stock**
1 tablespoon **dark soy sauce**
2 tablespoons **mirin**
3 tablespoons **sunflower oil**
1 tablespoon **sesame oil**
bunch of **scallions**, thickly
   sliced
2 **garlic cloves**, chopped
1 inch piece of **fresh ginger
   root**, peeled and grated
2 cups **risotto rice**
6 **kaffir lime leaves**
8 oz **shiitake mushrooms**,
   wiped and stems discarded
⅓ cup chopped **cilantro**, plus
   extra sprigs to garnish

Bring the stock, soy sauce, and mirin to a simmer in a saucepan. Meanwhile, heat 2 tablespoons of the sunflower oil and the sesame oil in a separate saucepan, add the scallions, garlic, and ginger, and cook over high heat, stirring, for 1 minute. Stir in the rice and lime leaves and cook over low heat for 1 minute, until glossy.

Stir ⅔ cup of the stock mixture into the rice and simmer, stirring, until it is almost all absorbed. Add the stock, a little at a time, and simmer, stirring, until all but a ladleful has been absorbed. Meanwhile, slice all but a few of the mushrooms. Heat the remaining oil in a skillet, add the mushrooms, and cook over medium heat, stirring frequently, for 5 minutes, until golden.

Add the cilantro to the risotto with the sliced mushrooms and the remaining stock. Simmer, stirring frequently, until almost all the stock is absorbed and the rice is tender and cooked through. Serve garnished with the whole mushrooms and cilantro sprigs.

For coconut & chile risotto, heat 2 tablespoons oil in a saucepan, add 1 coarsely chopped leek, 1 sliced red bell pepper, 1 chopped garlic clove, and 1 finely chopped red chile, and cook, stirring, over medium heat for 4 minutes, until softened. Stir in 1½ cups risotto rice and 6 kaffir lime leaves, then pour in 1¼ cups vegan stock. Bring to a boil, then simmer, stirring, until the liquid is almost all absorbed. Add 1⅔ cups coconut milk with another ⅔ cup stock and simmer, stirring frequently, for another 15 minutes, until the liquid is almost all absorbed and the rice is tender. Stir in 1⅓ cups frozen corn kernels with the grated zest of 1 lime and heat through. Sprinkle with chopped cilantro.

salads &
sides

spinach & butternut salad

Serves **4**
Preparation time **20 minutes**
Cooking time **30 minutes**

1 **small butternut squash**,
  peeled, seeded, and cut
  into wedges
2 tablespoons **flaxseed oil**
1 cup **walnut halves**
1 tablespoon **maple syrup**
pinch of **sea salt flakes**
4 cups **baby spinach leaves**
salt and **black pepper**

Mustard dressing
1 tablespoon **white wine
  vinegar**
1 teaspoon **whole-grain
  mustard**
3 tablespoons **olive oil**
pinch of **sugar**
salt and **black pepper**

Toss the butternut squash with the flaxseed oil on a baking sheet and season with salt and black pepper. Spread out in a single layer and roast in a preheated oven, at 400°F, for 30 minutes, until tender and beginning to char in places.

Meanwhile, mix the walnuts and maple syrup together in a small bowl and spread out over a separate baking sheet lined with aluminum foil. Sprinkle with the salt flakes and bake in the oven for 5–7 minutes, until toasted and caramelized.

Put all the dressing ingredients in a screw-top jar and season with salt and black pepper. Screw on the lid and shake well to mix.

Transfer the roasted squash to a salad bowl and add the spinach. Pour the dressing over the salad and toss gently together. Sprinkle with the caramelized walnuts.

For endive, roasted pear & caramelized pecan salad, peel, core, and thickly slice 3 pears. Toss with 2 tablespoons flaxseed oil on a baking sheet, spread out in a single layer, and roast in a preheated oven, at 400°F), for 20 minutes, until tender. Meanwhile, mix 1 cup pecan halves and 1 tablespoon maple syrup together in a small bowl. Spread out over a separate baking sheet lined with aluminum foil, sprinkle with a pinch of sea salt flakes, and bake in the oven for 5–7 minutes, until toasted and caramelized. Prepare the mustard dressing as above. Put the leaves from 2 heads of endive in a serving dish. Top with the roasted pears, drizzle with ¼ cup of the mustard dressing, and sprinkle with the caramelized pecans.

roasted roots & quinoa salad

Serves **4**

Preparation time **10 minutes**

Cooking time **35–40 minutes**

2 cups **raw baby beets** (about
   10 oz), scrubbed, halved or
   quartered if large

10 oz **baby carrots**, scrubbed

1 tablespoon **olive oil**

1 teaspoon **cumin seeds**

1 cup **quinoa**, rinsed
   and drained

1 (15 oz) can **chickpeas**,
   drained

1 small **red onion**, thinly sliced

small handful of **mint leaves**,
   coarsely chopped

2 tablespoons **blanched
   hazelnuts**, coarsely chopped

juice of **1 lime**

1 tablespoon **tamari** or
   soy sauce

1 teaspoon **sesame oil**

salt and **black pepper**

Put the beets and carrots into a roasting pan. Drizzle with the olive oil, sprinkle with the cumin seeds, and season well with salt and black pepper, then toss until the roots are evenly coated in the oil. Roast in a preheated oven, at 400°F, for 30–35 minutes, until tender.

Meanwhile, cook the quinoa in a saucepan of boiling water for 10–12 minutes, or according to package directions, until tender, then drain. Transfer to a large bowl, add the chickpeas, onion, mint, and hazelnuts, and toss together.

Mix the lime juice, tamari or soy sauce, and sesame oil together in a small bowl, pour it over the quinoa mixture, and gently toss together. Add the roasted beets and carrots and lightly mix through.

For roasted carrot & parsnip salad with edamame,

toss 10 oz each of scrubbed baby carrots and baby parsnips with 1 tablespoon olive oil, 1 teaspoon cumin seeds, and salt and black pepper in a roasting pan. Roast in a preheated oven, at 400°F, for 20–25 minutes, until tender. Meanwhile, cook the quinoa as above, adding 1 cup frozen edamame (soybeans) for the final 3 minutes of the cooking time. Drain and transfer to a large bowl. Add 1 thinly sliced red onion, a handful of coarsely chopped flat leaf parsley, and 2 tablespoons toasted blanched almonds, coarsely chopped. Make the lime juice dressing as above, pour it over the quinoa mixture, and gently toss together. Add the roasted carrots and parsnips and lightly mix through.

new potato, basil & pine nut salad

Serves **4–6**
Preparation time **10 minutes**,
   plus cooling
Cooking time **15–18 minutes**

2 lb **new potatoes,** scrubbed
¼ cup **extra virgin olive oil**
1½ tablespoons **white wine
   vinegar**
⅓ cup **pine nuts**
½ bunch of **basil leaves**
salt and **black pepper**

Cook the potatoes in a large saucepan of lightly salted boiling water for 12–15 minutes, until tender. Drain well and transfer to a large bowl. Cut any large potatoes in half.

Whisk together the oil, vinegar, and a little salt and black pepper in a small bowl. Add half to the potatoes, stir well, and let cool completely.

Toast the pine nuts in a dry skillet over medium heat, shaking the pan occasionally, for 2–3 minutes until golden. Remove from the pan and let cool.

Add the toasted pine nuts, the remaining dressing, and the basil to the potatoes, toss well, and then serve.

broccoli, pea & avocado salad

Serves **4**
Preparation time **20 minutes**,
  plus cooling
Cooking time **5 minutes**

1 tablespoon **sesame seeds**
1 tablespoon **chia seeds**
5 cups **small broccoli florets**
1 cup **frozen peas**
1 large ripe **avocado**, peeled,
  pitted, and chopped
4 cups **baby spinach leaves**
1 cup **alfalfa sprouts**
2 tablespoons chopped **mint**
juice of 1 **lime**
2 teaspoons **sesame oil**
¾ inch piece of **fresh ginger
  root**, peeled and grated
salt and **black pepper**

Toast the sesame and chia seeds in a dry saucepan over medium heat, shaking the pan a couple of times, for 30 seconds, until golden. Remove from the pan and let cool.

Blanch the broccoli with the peas in a large saucepan of boiling water for 2 minutes, until the broccoli is just tender but still firm. Drain, rinse under cold water, and drain again.

Put the broccoli and peas into a large salad bowl. Add the avocado, spinach leaves, alfalfa, mint, and toasted seeds.

Whisk the lime juice, oil, and ginger together in a small bowl and season with salt and black pepper. Pour the dressing over the salad and toss well to mix.

For spinach, beet & pomegranate salad, toast the sesame and chia seeds as above. Put 4 cups baby spinach leaves in a salad bowl with 1¼ cups chopped marinated beets, 2 sliced celery sticks, 1 ripe large avocado, peeled, pitted, and chopped, 1 cup alfalfa sprouts, small handful of chopped flat leaf parsley leaves, and the toasted seeds. Make the lime juice dressing as above, then pour it over the salad and toss well to mix.

warm lentil, tomato & onion salad

Serves **4**
Preparation time **15 minutes**
Cooking time **40–45 minutes**

1 tablespoon **olive oil**
1 large **red onion**, thinly sliced
1 ½ inch **fresh ginger root**,
  peeled and chopped
4 **garlic cloves**, thinly sliced
⅔ cup **dried green lentils**,
  rinsed and drained
½ cup **dried red split lentils**,
  rinsed and drained
½ teaspoon **ground cinnamon**
3 fresh **tomatoes**, coarsely
  chopped, or 1 (14½ oz) can
  diced tomatoes
1 ½ cups **water** or
  vegetable stock
2 teaspoons **black**
  onion seeds
salt and **black pepper**
parsley leaves, to garnish

Heat the oil in a large, heavy saucepan, add the onion, ginger, and garli,c and cook over gentle heat, stirring frequently, for 10 minutes, until softened but not browned.

Stir the lentils, cinnamon, tomatoes, and measured water or stock into the pan, season with salt and black pepper and bring to a boil. Cover and simmer gently for 30–35 minutes, or until the lentils are tender and the liquid is absorbed.

Spoon the lentils into warm serving bowls, sprinkle with the black onion seeds, and garnish with parsley leaves. Serve warm with lemon wedges and toasted whole-wheat flatbreads, if desired.

For no-stove lentil, tomato & onion salad, heat 1 (8 oz) package precooked lentils in a microwave, following the package directions, or use leftover cooked lentils—you can use chilled without heating them. Put in a bowl and mix with ½ finely chopped red onion, 4 chopped tomatoes, 1 small crushed garlic clove, ½ inch piece of fresh ginger root, peeled and grated, and 2 tablespoons chopped flat leaf parsley. Whisk 2 tablespoons lemon juice, 1 tablespoon olive oil, and a pinch each of ground cinnamon and paprika together in a small bowl and season with salt and black pepper. Add the dressing to the lentil salad and toss to coat, then serve garnished with parsley leaves.

tamarind-dressed chinese salad

Serves **4**

Preparation time **20 minutes**

½ head of **napa cabbage**,
   trimmed and finely shredded
½ **large daikon radish**,
   peeled and shredded
4 **carrots**, peeled and
   shredded
¼ **cucumber**, halved
   lengthwise and thinly sliced
8 **scallions**, diagonally thinly
   sliced
1 **mango**, peeled, pitted, and
   cut into chunks
1 cup **raw unsalted cashew
   nuts**, toasted
handful of **cilantro leaves**

Dressing

½ cup **boiling water**
2 tablespoons **tamarind paste**
1 tablespoon **palm, demerara**
   or **other raw sugar**
1 **red chile**, thinly sliced
¼ cup **light soy sauce**
finely grated zest and juice
   of **1 lime**

Put the cabbage in a large bowl with the grated daikon and carrots and toss well to mix.

Add the cucumber, scallions, and mango to the bowl and toss again, then sprinkle with the cashews and cilantro leaves and give a final toss.

Pour the measured boiling water over the tamarind paste in a small small bowl and blend together with the back of a spoon until well mixed and the paste is dissolved. Add the sugar and stir until dissolved. Whisk in the chile, soy sauce, and lime zest and juice. Pour the dresssnig over the salad and toss well before serving.

For Thai peanut salad with chile & soy dressing,

toss ½ head of napa cabbage, trimmed and finely shredded, with 2 cups bean sprouts, 1 cored, seeded, and finely sliced red bell pepper, ¼ cucumber, halved lengthwise and thinly sliced, 1 peeled and shredded carrot, and 8 scallions, diagonally thinly sliced, in a large bowl. Add 1 cup salted peanuts and toss again. Whisk together 3 tablespoons light soy sauce, 2 tablespoons sesame oil, 3 tablespoons chopped cilantro, and 1 finely chopped red chile in a small bowl. Pour the dressing over the salad and toss well before serving.

mediterranean potato salad

Serves **4**

Preparation time **10 minutes**, plus cooling

Cooking time **20 minutes**

4 **red-skinned potatoes**, peeled and cut into chunks

pinch of **saffron threads**

1 cup drained **sun-dried tomatoes in oil**

¾ cup coarsely chopped **pitted black ripe olives**

⅓ cup **olive oil**

¼ cup **chia seeds**

⅓ cup chopped **basil leaves**

3 tablespoons **capers**

salt and **black pepper**

Add the potatoes to a medium saucepan, pour in just enough cold water to cover the potatoes, and add the saffron. Bring to a boil, then cover and simmer gently for 15 minutes, until tender and cooked through. Drain and let cool.

Put the sun-dried tomatoes, olives, oil, chia seeds, basil leaves, and capers in a large bowl, add the cooled potatoes, and gently toss together. Season with a little salt and plenty of black pepper.

Divide the salad among 4 serving bowls and serve with fresh crusty bread or a simple arugula salad, if desired.

For Mediterranean pasta salad, cook 8 oz dried pasta shapes in a large saucepan of lightly salted boiling water for 8–10 minutes, or according to package directions, until just tender. Drain well, rinse under cold water, and drain again. Put 1 cup coarsely chopped drained, sun-dried tomatoes in oil, ¾ cup coarsely chopped, pitted black ripe olives, ⅓ cup olive oil, ¼ cup chia seeds, ⅓ cup chopped basil leaves, and 3 tablespoons capers in a large bowl. Toss well so that all the ingredients are well mixed. Season with salt and black pepper before serving.

fennel, apple & red cabbage slaw

Serves **4**

Preparation time **20 minutes**

¼ **red cabbage**, shredded

1 **fennel bulb**, trimmed and
thinly sliced

1 **crisp, sweet apple**, cored
and thinly sliced

1 small **red onion**, thinly sliced

1 **celery stick**, sliced

2 tablespoons **sunflower
seeds**

2 tablespoons **pumpkin
seeds**

⅓ cup **vegan mayonnaise**

1 tablespoon **lemon juice**

1 teaspoon **Dijon mustard**

small handful of **flat leaf
parsley**, coarsely chopped

salt and **black pepper**

Put the cabbage in a large bowl, add the fennel, apple,
onion, celery, and sunflower and pumpkin seeds, and
toss well to combine.

Mix the mayonnaise, lemon juice, and mustard together
in a small bowl and season with salt and black pepper.
Add to the cabbage mixture with the parsley and gently
toss together to coat in the dressing.

For beet & celeriac slaw with horseradish dressing,

shred 1 peeled raw beet, ¼ peeled celeriac, and
1 peeled and cored apple into a bowl. Add ¼ shredded
red cabbage, 1 small red onion, thinly sliced, and
2 tablespoons each sunflower and pumpkin seeds.
Mix 3 tablespoons vegan mayonnaise, 1 tablespoon
lemon juice, and 1 teaspoon grated horseradish
together in a small bowl and season with salt and black
pepper. Add to the vegetables with a small handful of
coarsely chopped flat leaf parsley and toss well to mix.

roasted summer vegetables

Serves **4**
Preparation time **15 minutes**
Cooking time **45–50 minutes**

1 **red bell pepper**, cored,
   seeded, and thickly sliced
1 **yellow bell pepper**, cored,
   seeded, and thickly sliced
1 **eggplant**, trimmed and cut
   into chunks
2 **yellow** or **green zucchini**,
   trimmed and cut into chunks
1 **red onion**, cut into wedges
6 **garlic cloves**, peeled
2 tablespoons **extra virgin
   canola** or **olive oil**
4–5 **thyme sprigs**
8 **mixed yellow** and **red baby
   plum tomatoes**
1 cup **hazelnuts**
4 cups **arugula leaves**
2 tablespoons **raspberry** or
   balsamic vinegar
salt and **black pepper**
handful of **mustard cress**,
   to garnish (optional)

Toss all the vegetables, except the tomatoes, and the garlic cloves in a large bowl with the oil. Season with a little salt and black pepper and add the thyme. Put into a large roasting pan and roast in a preheated oven, at 375°F, for 40–45 minutes, or until the vegetables are tender. Add the tomatoes and return to the oven for another 5 minutes, or until the tomatoes are just softened and beginning to burst.

Meanwhile, put the hazelnuts into a small roasting pan and toast in the oven for 10–12 minutes, or until golden and the skins are peeling away. Let cool, then rub off the excess skin with a clean kitchen towel and lightly crush the nuts.

Toss the arugula leaves gently with the roasted vegetables and pile onto large plates. Sprinkle with the crushed hazelnuts and drizzle with the vinegar. Sprinkle with the mustard cress, if using, and serve immediately.

For roasted vegetable pasta sauce, roast all the vegetables, except the tomatoes, and the garlic cloves as above, then put into a saucepan with the tomatoes, 2 cups tomato puree or sauce, and ⅔ cup vegetable stock. Bring to a boil, then simmer gently for 20 minutes. Remove from the heat and use an immersion blender to blend until smooth. Season with salt and black pepper and serve over cooked pasta.

marinated tofu with crunchy salad

Serves **4**
Preparation time **20 minutes**,
  plus marinating
Cooking time **10 minutes**

8 oz **firm tofu**, drained
3 tablespoons **light soy sauce**
1 tablespoon **hoisin sauce**
1 tablespoon **sesame oil**
2 tablespoons chopped
  cilantro
1 small **red chile**, seeded
  and finely chopped
1 inch piece of **fresh ginger
  root**, peeled and grated
1¾ cups **bean sprouts**
6 **scallions**, cut into strips
¼ head of **napa cabbage**,
  trimmed and finely shredded
⅓ cup **salted peanuts**

Cut the tofu into 1 inch cubes, put in a bowl with
1 tablespoon of the soy sauce, the hoisin sauce,
sesame oil, cilantro, chile, and ginger, and gently toss
to mix. Cover and let marinate in the refrigerator for
2 hours or overnight.

Put the bean sprouts, scallions, cabbage, and peanuts
in a large bowl and toss well. Add the remaining
2 tablespoons soy sauce and toss to lightly coat.

Heat a ridged grill pan until hot, add the marinated
tofu, and cook over high heat, turning occasionally,
for 2–3 minutes, until lightly scorched on all sides.
Toss into the salad ingredients and serve.

For asian tofu with sesame seeds, cut 8 oz drained
firm tofu into 4 thin slices and marinate as above.
Remove from the marinade to a plate and sprinkle
2 teaspoons sesame seeds over both sides of the tofu
slices. Heat a ridged grill pan until hot, add the tofu,
and cook over medium heat for 1–2 minutes on each
side, until scorched. Toss 1¼ cups bean sprouts and
2 thinly sliced scallions with 1 tablespoon dark soy
sauce in a bowl, then divide among 4 small plates
and top with the hot tofu. Sprinkle with 1 tablespoon
chopped cilantro and serve as a salad appetizer.

asparagus with sesame dressing

Serves **4**
Preparation time **15 minutes**
Cooking time **15 minutes**

3 bunches of **asparagus**
   spears, trimmed
¼ cup **olive oil**

Dressing
¼ cup **sesame seeds**
¼ cup **tahini**
finely grated zest and juice of
   1 **lemon**
3 tablespoons **light soy sauce**
2 tablespoons **mirin**
¼ cup **water**

Lay the asparagus spears in a roasting pan, drizzle with 2 tablespoons of the oil, and toss until evenly coated in the oil. Roast in a preheated oven, at 425°F, for 15 minutes, until tender and lightly charred in places.

Meanwhile, toast the sesame seeds in a dry skillet over medium heat, shaking the pan occasionally, for about 2 minutes, until golden. Transfer to a small bowl with the tahini, lemon zest and juice, soy sauce, mirin, and the measured water. Add the remaining olive oil, then use an immersion blender to blend until smooth.

Spoon half the dressing over the roasted asparagus and toss well to coat. Arrange on 4 serving plates and serve the remaining dressing separately.

For roasted baby carrots with tahini & sesame dip, put 12 oz scrubbed baby carrots in a roasting pan, drizzle with 1 tablespoon olive oil, and toss until evenly coated in the oil. Roast in a preheated oven, at 425°F, for 20 minutes, until just tender and lightly charred in places. To make the dip, put ¼ cup tahini into a small bowl with the finely grated zest of 1 lemon and 2 tablespoons each light soy sauce and toasted sesame seeds. Use an immersion blender to blend until smooth. Transfer to a small serving bowl and place on a serving platter. Arrange the roasted carrots around the bowl for dipping, once cool enough to handle.

red pepper & eggplant hummus

Serves **4–6**
Preparation time **10 minutes**,
  plus cooling
Cooking time **50 minutes**

1 **red bell pepper**, cored,
  seeded, and quartered
3 **garlic cloves**, unpeeled
  and lightly crushed
1 **eggplant**, trimmed and cut
  into large chunks
1 tablespoon **chili oil**, plus
  extra to serve
½ tablespoon **fennel seeds**
  (optional)
1 (15 oz) can **chickpeas**,
  drained
1 tablespoon **tahini**
1 teaspoon **sesame seeds**,
  lightly toasted
salt and **black pepper**

To serve
4 **whole-wheat pita breads**
olive oil spray
1 teaspoon **paprika**
salt

Arrange the red bell pepper, garlic cloves, and eggplant in a single layer in a large roasting pan. Drizzle with the chili oil, sprinkle with the fennel seeds, if using, and season with salt and black pepper. Roast in a preheated oven, at 375°F, for 35–40 minutes, or until softened and golden. Remove from the oven but do not turn it off.

Squeeze the soft garlic out of its skin and put in a blender or food processor with the roasted vegetables, three-quarters of the chickpeas, and the tahini. Blend until almost smooth, season with salt and black pepper, and then spoon into a serving bowl. Cover with plastic wrap and let cool.

Cut the pita breads into 1 inch strips and put into a large bowl. Spray with a little olive oil and toss with the paprika and a little salt until well coated. Spread out in a single layer on a baking sheet. Toast in the oven for 10–12 minutes, or until crisp.

Sprinkle the hummus with the remaining chickpeas and the sesame seeds and drizzle with 1–2 tablespoons chili oil. Serve with the toasted pita breads.

For roasted artichoke & red pepper hummus,
roast the red pepper and garlic cloves as above with 1 drained (14 oz) can artichoke hearts in water instead of the eggplant, using 1 tablespoon lemon-infused oil in place of the chili oil and omitting the fennel seeds. Continue with the recipe above to make the hummus and toast the pita breads.

mushrooms with salsa verde

Serves **4**
Preparation time **20 minutes**
Cooking time **10 minutes**

1 tablespoon **red wine
   vinegar**
1 teaspoon **sugar**
finely grated zest and juice
   of 1 **lemon**
⅓ cup **olive oil**
1 **garlic clove**, finely chopped
2 tablespoons chopped
   parsley
2 tablespoons chopped **basil**
1 tablespoon **capers**, finely
   chopped
4 **portobello mushrooms**,
   trimmed
salt and **black pepper**
4 slices of **walnut bread**,
   lightly toasted, to serve

Put the vinegar in a small bowl with the sugar, lemon zest and juice, 2 tablespoons of the oil, the garlic, parsley, basil, and capers. Mix together well and season with a little salt and plenty of black pepper.

Heat the remaining 3 tablespoons oil in a large, heavy skillet, add the mushrooms, and cook over high heat, turning once, for 5–6 minutes, until softened.

Turn the mushrooms out onto 4 small, warm serving plates, spoon the salsa verde over them, and serve with toasted walnut bread.

For roasted peppers with salsa verde, cut 2 red bell peppers in half lengthwise and remove the core and seeds but keep the stem intact. Place the bell pepper halves, cut side down, in a roasting pan, drizzle with 1 tablespoon olive oil, and roast in a preheated oven, at 400°F, for 20–25 minutes, until soft. Make the salsa verde as above and spoon it over the roasted peppers on 4 small, warm serving plates. Serve with lightly toasted Mediterranean bread.

onion bhajis with mango chutney

Serves **4**
Preparation time **20 minutes**
Cooking time **15 minutes**

2 teaspoons **cumin seeds**, toasted
½ teaspoon **ground turmeric**
1 teaspoon **ground coriander**
small handful of **cilantro leaves**, coarsely chopped
1 **green chile**, seeded and finely chopped
1 large **onion**, halved and sliced
1⅔ cups **chickpea (besan) flour**
vegetable oil, for deep-frying

Chutney
1 large ripe **mango**, peeled and pitted
½ **red chile**, seeded
1 teaspoon **black onion seeds**, toasted
1 teaspoon packed **light brown sugar**
1 teaspoon **white wine vinegar**
2 teaspoons **canola oil**
½ teaspoon **ground coriander**
leaves from a few **mint sprigs**
salt and **black pepper**

Pulse all the chutney ingredients, except the seasoning, together in a food processor until finely chopped. Season with salt and black pepper and transfer to a serving bowl.

Put the cumin seeds, turmeric, ground and fresh cilantro, chile, and onion in a bowl. Stir to mix, then sprinkle with the flour and add enough cold water to bind the mixture together. The batter needs to be thick enough to hold its shape in spoonfuls.

Fill a deep pan halfway with vegetable oil and heat to 350–375°F, or until a cube of bread browns in 30 seconds. Drop spoonfuls of the batter, about the size of a golf ball, in batches, into the oil and fry for 3–4 minutes, until golden and crisp. Remove from the pan with a slotted spoon, drain on paper towels, and keep warm in a low oven. Serve warm with the chutney.

For cabbage & parsnip bhajis with coconut mango chutney, pulse together 1 large ripe mango, peeled and pitted, 2 tablespoons coarsely grated fresh coconut or 1 tablespoon unsweetened dried coconut, ½ seeded red chile, 2 teaspoons canola oil, 1 teaspoon each light brown sugar, black onion seeds, and white wine vinegar, ½ teaspoon ground coriander, and a few cilantro leaves in a food processor until finely chopped. Season with salt and black pepper and transfer to a bowl. Mix together 2 teaspoons each toasted cumin seeds and garam masala, 2 tablespoons coarsely chopped cilantro leaves, 1 chopped green chile, 1 cup shredded cabbage, and 1 large peeled and shredded parsnip in a bowl. Sprinkle with 1½ cups chicken (besan) flour and continue as above to make and deep-fry the bhajis. Serve with the chutney.

bean, lemon & rosemary hummus

Serves **4–6**
Preparation time **10 minutes**,
  plus cooling
Cooking time **10 minutes**

⅓ cup **extra virgin olive oil**,
  plus extra to serve
4 **shallots**, finely chopped
2 large **garlic cloves**, crushed
1 teaspoon chopped
  rosemary, plus extra sprigs
  to garnish
finely grated zest and juice
  of ½ **lemon**
2 (15 oz) cans **lima beans**,
  drained
salt and **black pepper**
toasted **ciabatta**, to serve

Heat the oil in a skillet, add the shallots, garlic, chopped rosemary, and lemon zest and cook over gentle heat, stirring occasionally, for 10 minutes, until the shallots are softened. Let cool.

Transfer the shallot mixture to a blender or food processor, add all the remaining ingredients, and blend until smooth.

Spread the hummus onto toasted ciabatta, garnish with rosemary sprigs, and serve drizzled with oil.

For chickpea & chile dip, put 2 (15 oz) cans chickpeas, drained, 2 seeded and chopped red chiles, 1 large garlic clove, crushed, 2 tablespoons lemon juice, and salt and black pepper in a blender or food processor and add enough extra virgin olive oil to blend to a soft paste. Serve as a dip with vegetable sticks.

breads & baking

chile & zucchini foccacia

Serves **6**

Preparation time **30 minutes**, plus rising

Cooking time **30–35 minutes**

3⅔ cups **white bread flour**, plus extra for dusting

2¼ teaspoons **active dry yeast** (¼ oz envelope)

1 teaspoon **salt**

¼ cup **olive oil**, plus extra for oiling

1 cup, plus 2 tablespoons **warm water**

½ small **onion**, thinly sliced

½ small **zucchini**, trimmed and thinly sliced

1 **red chile**, seeded and thinly sliced

1 teaspoon **sea salt flakes**

a few small **rosemary sprigs**

Sift the flour into a bowl. Add the yeast to one side and the salt to the other side. Add 2 tablespoons of the oil and the measured water and mix to form a dough, adding a little more water if the dough seems dry.

Turn out the dough onto a lightly floured surface and knead for 10 minutes, until smooth and stretchy. Put the dough in a clean bowl, cover with plastic wrap, and let rise in a warm place for about 1 hour, until doubled in size.

Turn the dough out onto a lightly floured surface and knead lightly for 1 minute. Press or roll the dough out to a rough oblong about ½ inch thick and place on a lightly oiled baking sheet. Loosely cover and let rise for 20 minutes.

Meanwhile, heat 1 tablespoon of the remaining oil in a skillet, add the onion, and cook over medium heat for about 3 minutes, until just softened. Add the zucchini and chile and cook for another 3 minutes. Set aside.

Press indentations with your fingertip into the dough surface. Drizzle with the remaining oil and bake in a preheated oven, at 400°F, for 10 minutes. Sprinkle the vegetable mixture over the top with the salt flakes and rosemary sprigs and bake for another 10–15 minutes, until golden. Cool on a wire rack.

For potato, onion & thyme focaccia, make the dough as above. While it is rising, sauté 1 small sliced onion and 1 large baking potato, scrubbed and thinly sliced, in 1 tablespoon oil over medium heat for 5–8 minutes, until tender. Bake as above, adding the onion and potato slices instead of the vegetable mixture, and adding thyme sprigs instead of rosemary.

olive & tomato bread

Makes **1 large loaf**
Preparation time
 1¾–2¾ hours, depending
 on machine, plus rising
Cooking time **30 minutes**

Dough
1 cup, plus 2 tablespoons
 water
2 tablespoons **olive oil**,
 plus extra for oiling
1 teaspoon **salt**
3½ cups **white bread flour**,
 plus extra for dusting
1 teaspoon **sugar**
1¼ teaspoons **active
 dry yeast**

To finish
1¼ cups pitted or stuffed
 green olives, coarsely
 chopped
5 pieces **sun-dried tomatoes**
 (not in oil), coarsely chopped
sea salt flakes and **paprika**,
 for sprinkling

Lift the bread pan out of a bread-making machine and fit the blade. Put all the dough ingredients in the pan, following the order specified in the machine's manual.

Fit the pan into the machine and close the lid. Set to the dough program.

Turn out the dough onto a lightly floured surface at the end of the program. Gradually work in the olives and sun-dried tomatoes. Pat the dough into an 8 inch circle and use a floured knife to mark it into 8 wedges. Do not cut right through to the bottom.

Sprinkle salt flakes and paprika over the dough, transfer to a large, lightly oiled baking sheet, cover loosely with oiled plastic wrap, and let rise in a warm place for 30 minutes, until it is half as big again.

Bake in a preheated oven, at 400°F, for 30 minutes. Check after 15 minutes and cover with aluminum foil if overbrowning. Transfer to a wire rack to cool.

For paprika, Peppadew, black olive & rosemary bread, prepare the bread dough as above, adding 2 teaspoons paprika to the flour. At the end of the dough program, turn out the dough onto a lightly floured surface and knead in ½ cup drained and coarsely chopped Peppadew peppers or pimentos, ¾ cup coarsely chopped, pitted black ripe olives, and 1 tablespoon chopped rosemary. Pat into a circle and mark into wedges as above. Sprinkle with 1 teaspoon sea salt flakes and transfer to a lightly oiled baking sheet. Let rise, bake, and cool as above.

herb & walnut rye soda bread

Serves **6**

Preparation time **15 minutes**, plus standing

Cooking time **40–45 minutes**

2 cups **rye flour**

½ cup coarsely chopped **walnuts**, plus 1 tablespoon coarsely chopped for sprinkling

¼ cup chopped **mixed herbs**, such as rosemary, parsley, or thyme

1 teaspoon **baking soda**

2 teaspoons **xanthan gum**

¼ teaspoon **salt**

1 cup **rice milk**

2 tablespoons **canola oil**, plus extra for oiling

Mix together the flour, walnuts, mixed herbs, baking soda, xanthan gum, and salt in a large bowl, then make a well in the center. Whisk together the rice milk and canola oil in a small bowl, then pour most of it into the well and stir in with a wooden spoon until a soft, slightly sticky dough is formed, adding more if needed.

Turn out the dough onto a lightly floured surface and pat into a 7 inch circle. Place onto a baking sheet. Sprinkle with the extra walnuts and gently press to adhere to the dough. Make a deep cross in the dough with a sharp knife, then let stand in a warm place for 30 minutes.

Bake in a preheated oven, at 425°F, for 40–45 minutes, until the bread is crisp on the outside and cooked through; the bottom should sound hollow when tapped with the fingertips. Turn out onto a wire rack to cool before slicing thickly to serve.

For pumpkin & sunflower seed whole-wheat soda bread, mix together 2 cups whole-wheat all-purpose flour, 1 teaspoon baking soda, 2 teaspoons xanthan gum, and ¼ cup each sunflower seeds and pumpkin seeds in a large bowl. Make a well in the center. Continue with the recipe as above, adding the rice milk and canola oil to make a dough and preparing it on the baking sheet for baking. After cutting the cross in the dough, sprinkle with an extra tablespoon pumpkin seeds and let rest in a warm place for 30 minutes. Bake, cool, and serve as above.

pita breads

Makes **8 breads**

Preparation time
 1¾–2¾ hours, depending
 on machine, plus rising

Cooking time **10–12 minutes**

1 cup **water**

1 tablespoon **olive oil**

1 teaspoon **salt**

½ teaspoon ground **cumin**

2¾ cups **white bread flour**,
 plus extra for dusting

1 teaspoon **sugar**

1 teaspoon **active dry yeast**

Lift the bread pan out of a bread-making machine and fit the blade. Put the ingredients in the pan, following the order specified in the machine's manual.

Fit the pan into the machine and close the lid. Set to the dough program.

Turn out the dough onto a lightly floured surface at the end of the program and cut it into 8 equal pieces. Roll out each piece to an oval about 6 inches long. Arrange in a single layer on a well-floured clean, dry kitchen towel. Cover loosely with a second clean, dry kitchen towel and let rise in a warm place for 30 minutes.

Put a floured baking sheet in a preheated oven, at 450°F, and let heat up for 5 minutes. Transfer half the breads to the baking sheet and cook for 5–6 minutes, until just beginning to brown. Remove from the oven and let cool on a wire rack while you cook the remainder. Wrap the warm pita breads in a clean, dry kitchen towel to keep them soft until ready to serve. If they are allowed to get cold, warm the pita breads in a hot oven before serving.

For olive & herb mini pita breads, make the dough as above, adding ½ cup chopped, pitted black ripe olives and a large handful of chopped parsley and mint to the dough when the machine beeps. Turn the out dough onto a lightly floured surface at the end of the program and cut it into 16 pieces. Roll out each piece thinly to an oval 4–5 inches long. Let rise and then bake as above.

mini parsnip & parsley loaves

Makes **10 loaves**

Preparation time
1¾–2¾ hours, depending
on machine, plus cooling
and risng

Cooking time **20–25 minutes**

1 cup peeled **parsnip chunks**

2 tablespoons **olive oil**, plus
extra for oiling

large pinch of **saffron threads**,
crumbled

1½ teaspoons **salt**

3⅓ cups **white bread flour**,
plus extra for dusting

1 teaspoon **sugar**

1¼ teaspoons **active dry
yeast**

¼ cup chopped **parsley**

1 medium-strength **red chile**,
seeded and thinly sliced

soy or other nondairy milk,
for brushing

Cook the parsnips in a saucepan of boiling water for 10 minutes, until just tender. Drain, reserving the liquid, return to the pan, and mash. Let cool.

Measure 1 cup plus 2 tablespoons of the reserved cooking liquid. Lift the bread pan out of a bread-making machine and fit the blade. Put the all the ingredients except the parsley, chile, and milk in the pan, following the order specified in the machine's manual. Add the mashed parsnips with the liquid. Fit the pan into the machine and close the lid. Set to the dough program, adding the parsley and chile when the machine beeps.

Turn out the dough onto a lightly floured surface at the end of the program and cut it into 10 equal pieces. Shape each piece of dough into a ball and drop into an oiled ⅔ cup dariole mold. Place the molds on a baking sheet and cover loosely with oiled plastic wrap. Let rest in a warm place for 25–30 minutes, or until the dough has just risen above the tops of the molds.

Brush the dough with the milk and bake in a preheated oven, at 425°F, for 10–15 minutes, until golden and the bottoms of the bread sound hollow when tapped. Transfer to a wire rack to cool.

For carrot & onion loaves, boil 1⅓ cups peeled and coarsely chopped carrots until just tender. Drain and mash, reserving 1 cup plus 2 tablespoons of the cooking liquid. Sauté 1 small onion, chopped, in 1 tablespoon oil over medium heat for 10 minutes, until soft. Make the bread as above, using 1¾ cups white bread flour and 1⅔ cups whole-wheat flour in place of the white flour and the carrots and their liquid instead of the parsnips.

artichoke & roasted pepper pizza

Makes **2**

Preparation time **20 minutes**,
  plus proving

Cooking time **15 minutes**

1²/₃ cups **white bread flour**,
  plus extra for dusting

2¼ teaspoons **active dry
  yeast** (¼ oz envelope)

pinch of **salt**

3 tablespoons **olive oil**

just under ⅔ cup **warm water**

⅔ cup **tomato puree or
  sauce**

1 **garlic clove**, crushed

1 teaspoon **oregano leaves**

1 tablespoon **semolina**

1 roasted **red pepper** from a
  can or jar, cut into wide strips

⅔ (14 oz) jar marinated
  artichokes in oil, drained

½ cup **black ripe olives**

4 oz **vegan mozzarella-style
  cheese**, shredded

2 handfuls of **arugula leaves**

salt and **black pepper**

Sift the flour into a bowl. Add the yeast to one side of
the bowl and the salt to the other. Add 2 tablespoons
of the oil and the measured water and mix to form a
dough, adding a little more water if the dough feels dry.

Turn out the dough onto a lightly floured surface and
knead for about 5 minutes, until smooth and stretchy.
Put the dough in a clean bowl, cover with plastic wrap,
and let rise in a warm place for about 20 minutes.

Meanwhile, mix the tomato puree or sauce, garlic and
oregano in a bowl and season with salt and black pepper.

Turn out the dough onto a lightly floured surface and
cut in half. Knead each piece lightly into a ball and roll
out thinly to a 10 inch circle. Place each circle on a
large baking sheet sprinkled with the semolina.

Spread the tomato puree or sauce mixture over
the dough circles and arrange the red pepper strips,
artichokes, and olives over the top in a thin layer.
Sprinkle with the vegan cheese, drizzle with the
remaining 1 tablespoon oil, and bake in a preheated
oven, at 425°F, for 12–15 minutes, until the bottoms are
crisp and golden. Top with arugula just before serving.

For zucchini, harissa & red onion pizza, make
2 pizza crusts and place each on a baking sheet
sprinkled with semolina as above. Mix 1 cup plus
2 tablespoons tomato puree or sauce with 1 teaspoon
harissa, spread over the pizza crusts, and top with
1 trimmed and thinly sliced zucchini and 1 thinly sliced
red onion. Sprinkle with ½ cup black ripe olives and 4 oz
shredded vegan mozzarella-style cheese, then bake as
above. Sprinkle with cilantro leaves before serving.

minted zucchini & lemon loaf

Makes **1 large loaf**
Preparation and cooking time
   3–4 hours, depending on
   machine, plus standing

1 large **zucchini**, trimmed
2 tablespoons **salt**, plus
   ½ teaspoon
¾ cup **water**
⅓ cup **olive oil**
½ teaspoon freshly ground
   black pepper
3 cups **white bread flour**
1 tablespoon **sugar**
1¼ teaspoons **active**
   dry yeast
finely grated zest of 1 **lemon**
2 tablespoons chopped **mint**
3 tablespoons **capers**, rinsed
   and drained

Shred the zucchini and mix in a colander with the
2 tablespoons salt. Let stand for 30 minutes. Rinse
the zucchini in plenty of cold water, pat dry between
several layers of paper towels, and set aside.

Lift the bread pan out of a bread-making machine and
fit the blade. Put all the ingredients except the lemon
zest, mint, and capers in the pan, following the order
specified in the machine's manual.

Fit the pan into the machine and close the lid. Set to a
1½ lb loaf size on the basic white program. Select your
preferred crust setting. Add the zucchini, lemon zest,
mint, and capers when the machine beeps.

Remove the pan from the machine at the end of
the program and shake the bread out onto a wire
rack to cool.

For carrot & spelt loaf with sesame, prepare the
bread dough as above, using 1 large carrot, peeled and
shredded, in place of the zucchini and using a mixture
of 2 cups white bread flour and 1 cup spelt flour
instead of all white bread flour. Set the bread-making
machine as above, then when the machine beeps,
add 3 tablespoons black or white sesame seeds and
2 tablespoons chopped parsley and proceed as above.

chocolate & beet fudge cake

Serves **12**

Preparation time **20 minutes**,
plus cooling and chilling

Cooking time **45–50 minutes**

2 cups **all-purpose flour**

1 cup **unsweetened cocoa powder**

1 teaspoon **baking soda**

1½ cups firmly packed **light brown sugar**

1¾ cups chopped **cooked fresh beet** (not pickled)

1¼ cups **almond milk**

½ cup **sunflower oil**, plus extra for oiling

2 teaspoons **vanilla extract**

1 tablespoon **cider vinegar**

pink **edible sprinkles** or fresh unsprayed **rose petals**, washed and patted dry, to decorate

Frosting

⅔ cup **vegan spread**

1¾ cups **confectioners' sugar**

1 teaspoon **vanilla extract**

5 oz **dairy-free semisweet chocolate**, melted (see page 232) and cooled

Sift together the flour, cocoa powder, and baking soda into a large bowl. Stir in the brown sugar.

Blend the beet in a blender or food processor until smooth. With the motor running, pour in the almond milk, oil, vanilla, and vinegar.

Pour the beet mixture onto the dry ingredients and stir until mixed. Pour into an oiled 8 inch springform cake that has a bottom lined with parchment paper and bake in a preheated oven, at 350°F, for 45–50 minutes, until just firm to the touch. Let cool in the pan.

Meanwhile, for the frosting, beat together the spread, confectioners' sugar, and vanilla until soft, then gradually beat in the melted chocolate until well combined and smooth. Refrigerate for 1 hour. Release the cooled cake from the pan, spread with the chilled frosting, and decorate with sprinkles or rose petals.

For double chocolate & zucchini sheet cake, sift together 2 cups all-purpose flour, 1 cup cocoa powder, and 1 teaspoon baking soda into a large bowl. Stir in 1½ cups firmly packed light brown sugar. Mix together 1¼ cups each almond milk and sunflower oil, 2 teaspoons vanilla extract, and 1 tablespoon cider vinegar in a small bowl. Shred 1 zucchini, squeezing out any excess moisture. Stir into the dry ingredients with the almond milk mixture and 4 oz dairy-free semisweet chocolate drops. Pour into an oiled and lined 7 x 11 inch shallow baking pan and bake in a preheated oven, at 350°F, for 25–30 minutes, until just firm to the touch. Cut into squares and dust with confectioners' sugar.

lemon & poppy seed cupcakes

Makes **12**

Preparation time **40 minutes**, plus cooling

Cooking time **20 minutes**

1¾ cups **all-purpose flour**

2 teaspoons **baking powder**

¼ teaspoon **baking soda**

½ teaspoon **salt**

⅔ cup **granulated sugar**

finely grated zest of 2 **lemons** and 1 tablespoon **lemon juice**

1 tablespoon **poppy seeds**, plus 1 teaspoon for decorating

⅓ cup **sunflower oil**

½ cup **rice milk**

Frosting

½ cup **vegan spread**

2 cups **confectioners' sugar**

finely grated zest of 1 **lemon**

a few drops of **yellow food coloring**

Sift together the flour, baking powder, baking soda, and salt into a large bowl. Stir in the sugar, lemon zest, and poppy seeds.

Mix together the oil, rice milk, and lemon juice in a small bowl. Add to the dry ingredients and stir to mix. Spoon evenly into a 12-section muffin pan lined with paper liners and bake in a preheated oven, at 325°F, for 15 minutes, until just firm to the touch. Let cool on a wire rack.

Beat together the spread, confectioners' sugar, lemon zest, and food coloring until soft and smooth to make the frosting. Spoon or pipe the frosting onto the cooled cakes and sprinkle with the remaining poppy seeds.

For rosewater & pistachio cupcakes, sift together 1¾ cups all-purpose flour, 2 teaspoons baking powder, ¼ teaspoon baking soda, and ½ teaspoon salt into a large bowl. Stir in ⅔ cup granulated sugar and ⅓ cup finely chopped pistachio nuts. Mix together ⅓ cup sunflower oil, ¼ cup rice milk, 1 tablespoon cider vinegar, and 1 teaspoon rosewater in a small bowl. Add to the dry ingredients and stir to mix. Spoon evenly into a 12-section muffin pan lined with paper liners and bake as above. Let cool on a wire rack. Beat together ½ cup vegan spread, 1¾ cups confectioners' sugar, and ½ teaspoon rosewater in an electric mixer or in a bowl until soft and smooth. Spread or pipe over the cooled cupcakes and sprinkle with chopped pistachios to decorate.

sticky cinnamon & pecan swirls

Makes **10**

Preparation time **45 minutes**, plus standing, rising, and setting

Cooking time **30 minutes**

1 tablespoon ground **flaxseed**

1 cup **almond milk**

4½ teaspoons **active dry yeast** (two ¼ oz envelopes)

3⅓ cups **white bread flour**, plus extra for dusting

½ teaspoon **salt**

⅓ cup **vegan spread**, cubed

¼ cup firmly packed **light brown sugar**

1 cup **confectioners' sugar**

sunflower oil, for oiling

Filling

½ cup **vegan spread**

½ cup firmly packed **light brown sugar**

2 teaspoons **ground cinnamon**

¾ cup coarsely chopped **pecans**

6 fresh **Medjool dates**, pitted and mashed

2 tablespoons **maple syrup**

Mix the flaxseed with 3 tablespoons water in a small bowl and set aside. Heat the almond milk gently in a saucepan until lukewarm. Stir in the yeast and let stand for 10 minutes.

Combine the flour and salt in a large bowl, add the spread, and rub in with the fingertips until the mixture resembles fine bread crumbs, then stir in the brown sugar. Mix the flaxseed mixture into the yeast mixture, then stir into the flour mixture and mix to a smooth, soft dough.

Turn out the dough onto a lightly floured surface and knead for about 5 minutes, until smooth and elastic. Put in a clean bowl, cover with plastic wrap, and let rise in a warm place for 10 minutes.

Mix together the spread, sugar, and cinnamon for the filling in a bowl until well combined. Add the pecans, mashed dates, and maple syrup and mix well.

Turn out the dough onto a lightly floured surface and knead for 2 minutes, until smooth. Roll out to a rectangle about 12 x 18 inches. Spread the filling evenly over the surface, then roll up tightly from one of the longer sides of the dough to form a spiral. Slice into 10 even slices, then place well spaced apart on a baking sheet, cover loosely with lightly oiled plastic wrap and let rise in a warm place for 30 minutes.

Remove the plastic wrap and bake in a preheated oven, at 400°F, for 25 minutes, until golden. Let cool on a wire rack. Mix the confectioners' sugar with 2 tablespoons water in a bowl until soft and smooth. Drizzle it over the cooled swirls and let set for 20 minutes before serving.

vanilla & jelly shortbread

Makes **8**

Preparation time **30 minutes**, plus chilling

Cooking time **10–12 minutes**

½ cup **vegan spread**

¼ cup **granulated sugar**

1 ¼ cups **all-purpose flour**, plus extra for dusting

3 tablespoons **cornstarch**

1 teaspoon **vanilla extract**

3 tablespoons **raspberry** or **strawberry jelly or jam**

confectioners' sugar, for dusting

Beat the spread and granulated sugar together in an electric mixer until pale and fluffy. Sift the flour and cornstarch together into the mixture, add the vanilla, and mix until combined. Roll the dough into a ball, wrap in plastic wrap, and chill for 30 minutes.

Roll out the dough on a lightly floured surface to about ¼ inch thick. Use a 2 inch square or round cutter to cut out 16 squares or circles, rerolling the scraps as necessary. Place on 2 baking sheets lined with parchment paper and bake in a preheated oven, at 325°F, for 10–12 minutes, until pale golden.

Let the shortbreads cool on the sheets for 10 minutes, until firm, then transfer to a wire rack to cool completely.

Sandwich the shortbreads together with the jelly or jam and dust with confectioners' sugar.

For jelly & coconut streusel tarts, make the shortbread dough and chill as above. Roll the dough out as above, then use a 3 inch round cutter to cut out 12 circles, rerolling the scraps as necessary. Use the circles to line 12 sections of a muffin pan. Add a teaspoonful of raspberry or strawberry jelly or jam to each lined section. Put 3 tablespoons all-purpose flour, ⅓ cup granulated sugar, ¼ cup vegan spread, and 3 tablespoons dried coconut into a bowl and rub together with the fingertips until crumbly. Sprinkle the topping over the jelly or jam and bake in a preheated oven, at 325°F, for 15 minutes, until golden.

cranberry scones & compote

Serves **6**

Preparation time **20 minutes**,
plus standing and cooling

Cooking time **25 minutes**

⅓ cup **soy milk**

1 tablespoon **cider vinegar**

1 tablespoon ground **flaxseed**

2¼ cups **all-purpose flour**,
plus extra for dusting

¼ cup **granulated sugar**

1 teaspoon **baking powder**

½ teaspoon **baking soda**

1 teaspoon ground **cinnamon**

½ cup **vegan spread**, cubed,
plus extra for greasing

1 cup **dried cranberries**

1 tablespoon **demerara** or
other raw sugar

Compote

1 cup hulled and quartered
strawberries

2 tablespoons **granulated
sugar**

1 cup **blackberries**

Mix together ⅓ cup of the soy milk, the vinegar, and flaxseed in a small bowl, then let stand for 10 minutes (the mixture will separate slightly and turn thick).

Meanwhile, heat the strawberries and sugar for the compote in a saucepan over gentle heat for 2–3 minutes, until the sugar is dissolved. Add the blackberries and cook for another 2–3 minutes, until the fruit has softened and a juice has formed. Remove from the heat and let cool.

Put the flour in a large bowl and stir in the granulated sugar, baking powder, baking soda, and cinnamon. Add the spread and rub in with the fingertips until the mixture resembles fine bread crumbs. Stir in the cranberries, then add the soy milk mixture and mix to a soft dough.

Roll out the dough on a lightly floured work surface to a 7 inch circle and score into 6 wedges with a knife. Place on a lightly greased baking sheet, brush with the remaining soy milk, and sprinkle with the demerara or other raw sugar. Bake in a preheated oven, at 400°F, for 15–18 minutes, until golden and cooked through. Let cool slightly, then serve warm with the cooled compote.

For lemon & blueberry scones, finely grate the zest of 1 lemon, then squeeze the juice. Mix together ⅓ cup soy milk, 1 tablespoon ground flaxseed, and the lemon juice in a small bowl, then let stand for 10 minutes. Make the dough as above, stirring in the lemon zest and 1 cup blueberries in place of the cranberries. Roll out on a lightly floured surface to an 8 inch circle and score into 6 wedges. Place on a lightly greased baking sheet and bake as above. Serve warm.

ginger & dark choc cookies

Makes **14**
Preparation time **20 minutes**
Cooking time **15 minutes**

⅓ cup **light corn syrup**
¼ cup **vegan spread**
1¼ cups **rolled oats**
⅔ cup **whole-wheat flour**
1 teaspoon **baking powder**
⅔ cup finely chopped, well-
    drained **preserved ginger**
    in syrup
2 oz **semisweet chocolate**,
    coarsely chopped

Heat the corn syrup and spread in a small saucepan over gentle heat until melted, stirring. Let cool slightly.

Mix all the remaining ingredients together in a large bowl. Pour in the syrup mixture and mix to form a soft dough. Place 14 spoonfuls of the dough well spaced apart on a large baking sheet lined with parchment paper and gently press with the back of a spoon to flatten slightly. Bake in a preheated oven, at 350°F, for 8–10 minutes, until pale golden.

Let the cookies cool on the baking sheet for 5 minutes, until firm, then transfer to a wire rack to cool completely.

For spiced hazelnut & raisin cookies, melt the corn syrup and vegan spread as above. Mix together ¾ cup eat rolled oats and whole-wheat all-purpose flour, ½ cup raisins, ⅓ cup lightly toasted and chopped hazelnuts, and 1 teaspoon each baking powder and ground allspice in a large bowl. Pour in the syrup mixture and mix to form a soft dough. Continue with the recipe above to form, bake, and cool the cookies.

sugarless fruit granola bars

Makes **9**

Preparation time **20 minutes**,
  plus cooling

Cooking time **40 minutes**

1 **large crisp, sweet apple**
  peeled, cored, and coarsely
  chopped

1 tablespoon **lemon juice**

1 tablespoon **agave syrup**

½ teaspoon ground **cinnamon**

sunflower oil, for oiling

Granola

1¼ cups **rolled oats**

1 cup **dried apricots**

5 fresh **Medjool dates**, pitted
  and coarsely chopped

2 tablespoons **ground
  flaxseed**

2 tablespoons **smooth
  peanut butter**

¼ cup **agave syrup**

Line a baking sheet with parchment paper. Toss the apple with the lemon juice, agave syrup, and cinnamon in a bowl, then spread out on the lined baking sheet and roast in a preheated oven, at 325°F, for 20 minutes. Remove from the oven and let cool.

Increase the oven temperature to at 350°F. Pulse all the ingredients for the granola together in a food processor a few times until mixed and mashed. Fold in the cooled roasted apple, then spoon into a lightly oiled 8 inch square, shallow cake pan and level with the back of a spoon. Bake in the oven for 20 minutes.

Let cool for 15 minutes before cutting into 9 squares to serve.

For pear, banana & hazelnut granola bars, toss 1 large peeled, cored, and chopped pear with 1 tablespoon each lemon juice and agave syrup in a bowl, then spread out on a baking sheet lined with parchment paper and roast in a preheated oven, at 350°F, for 20 minutes. Remove from the oven and let cool, keeping the oven on. Pulse together 1¼ cups rolled oats and 5 fresh Medjool dates, pitted and coarsely chopped, 1 small ripe banana, coarsely chopped, 2 tablespoons each ground flaxseed and toasted blanched hazelnuts, and ¼ cup agave syrup in a food processor a few times until mixed and mashed. Fold in the cooled roasted pear, then bake, cool, and cut into squares as above.

desserts

banana & strawberry ice cream

Serves **6**

Preparation time **30 minutes**, plus freezing

1¾ cups prepared **vanilla soy custard**

1 cup **soy cream**

3 **bananas**, coarsely chopped

1 cup hulled **strawberries**

3 tablespoons **maple syrup**

Blend together the custard, cream, bananas, half the strawberries, and the maple syrup in a blender or food processor until smooth.

Pour the mixture into a freezer-proof container and freeze for 3 hours, until just starting to freeze around the edges.

Scrape the mixture into a bowl and beat with an immersion blender until smooth. Finely chop the remaining strawberries, stir into the mixture, and pour back into the freezer-proof container. Freeze for 3–4 hours or overnight until firm. Let soften for 15 minutes before serving.

For choc chip banana ice cream, blend the vanilla soy custard, soy cream, and bananas as above with 2 tablespoons unsweetened cocoa powder. Partly freeze and then whisk until smooth as above. Stir in 3 oz semisweet chocolate chips before freezing until firm as above.

lemon & mint granita

Serves **6**
Preparation time **20 minutes**,
  plus cooling and freezing
Cooking time **5 minutes**

1 cup **granulated sugar**
1¼ cups **water**, plus extra
  to top up
pared zest and juice of
  3 **lemons**
½ cup **mint sprigs**, plus
  a few tiny sprigs for
  decorating
confectioners' sugar, for
  dusting

Heat the sugar, measured water, and lemon zest in a saucepan over gentle heat until the sugar is dissolved. Increase the heat and boil for 2 minutes, then remove the pan from the heat.

Tear the tips off the mint stems and finely chop to have about 3 tablespoons, then reserve. Add the larger mint leaves and stems to the hot syrup and let steep for 1 hour to cool and for the flavors to develop.

Strain the syrup through a strainer into a small bowl, add the chopped mint, and top up to 2½ cups with the lemon juice and extra cold water. Pour into a small roasting pan and freeze the mixture for 2–3 hours, or until mushy.

Break up the ice crystals with a fork, then return to the freezer for another 2–3 hours, breaking up with a fork once or twice more until the mixture is the consistency of crushed ice.

Spoon into glasses and decorate with tiny mint sprigs dusted with confectioners' sugar before serving, or leave in the freezer until required. If leaving in the freezer, let soften for 15 minutes before serving. If frozen overnight or longer, break up with a fork before serving.

For iced ruby grapefruit granita, make a plain sugar syrup as above, omitting the lemon zest, then let cool, omitting the mint. Halve 4 ruby grapefruits, squeeze the juice, and then reserve 4 of the grapefruit shell halves, scooping out and discarding any remaining flesh and membranes. Add the grapefruit juice to the syrup instead of the lemon juice, then freeze as above. Serve the granita spooned into the grapefruit shells.

lavender & rosemary sorbet

Serves **8**

Preparation time **25 minutes**,
plus cooling and freezing

Cooking time **30 minutes**

1 cup plus 2 tablespoons
granulated sugar

3½ cups **water**

⅓ cup **elderflower syrup**
or **cordial** (available online)

¼ cup **lavender flowers**

2 tablespoons **rosemary
leaves**

Put the sugar in a saucepan with the measured water, elderflower syrup or cordial, lavender, and rosemary and bring to a boil. Boil for 8–10 minutes, until the liquid has reduced by a third and become syrupy but without taking on any color. Remove from the heat and let cool completely.

Strain the cooled syrup through a strainer into a freezer-proof container and freeze for 4–5 hours, until firm. Remove from the freezer and cut into chunks, then use an immersion blender to beat until smooth. Return to the freezer and freeze again for 3–4 hours or overnight until firm. The sorbet is now ready to serve, but let soften for 15 minutes before serving.

For strawberry sorbet, make the syrup as above and let cool. Blend 3 cups hulled strawberries in a blender or food processor until smooth. Pour the syrup into the strawberries and mix well, then transfer to a freezer-proof container. Freeze, then beat until smooth and refreeze as above.

summer berry sorbet

Serves **2**

Preparation time **5 minutes**,
    plus freezing

2 cups **frozen mixed
    summer berries**, such as
    raspberries, strawberries,
    and/or **blueberries**

⅓ cup **spiced berry syrup**

2 tablespoons **Kirsch**

1 tablespoon **lime juice**

Put a shallow plastic container in the freezer to chill.
Process the frozen berries, syrup, Kirsch, and lime juice
in a food processor or blender to a smooth puree. Be
careful not to overprocess, because this will soften the
mixture too much.

Spoon into the chilled container and freeze for at least
25 minutes. Spoon into serving bowls and serve

For raspberry sorbet, replace the main recipe
ingredients with frozen raspberries, elderflower syrup
or cordial (available online), crème de cassis, and lemon
juice. Use the same quantities and method as the
summer berry sorbet.

melon, ginger & lime sorbet

Serves **4**

Preparation time **15 minutes**, plus cooling and freezing

1 large ripe **honeydew melon** or **canteloupe**, chilled
¾ cup **granulated sugar**
1 teaspoon peeled and finely grated **fresh ginger root**
juice of 2 **limes**

Cut the melon in half and remove and discard the seeds, then coarsely chop the flesh; you need about 3 cups. Place in a food processor with the sugar, ginger, and lime juice, then blend until smooth.

Transfer the sorbet to an ice cream maker and process according to the manufacturer's instructions. If you don't have an ice cream maker, place the mixture in a freezer-proof container and freeze for 2–3 hours or until ice crystals have appeared on the surface. Beat with a handheld electric mixer until smooth, then return to the freezer. Repeat this process twice more until you have a fine-textured sorbet and freeze until firm.

Remove the sorbet from the freezer 10 minutes before serving. Serve, scooped into glasses with a thin cookie.

For plain melon granita, put ⅓ cup granulated sugar in a saucepan with ⅔ cup water and stir over low heat until dissolved, then bring to a boil. Remove from the heat and let cool, then place in a food processor with 3 cups chopped honeydew melon or canteloupe flesh and 2 tablespoons melon liqueur (optional) and blend until smooth. Transfer to a shallow freezer-proof container and freeze for 1 hour or until ice crystals appear at the edges. Stir the ice into the center and return to the freezer. Stir and refreeze a few more times until frozen all over. To serve, scrape the granita with a fork and serve immediately.

spiced baked figs

Serves **4**
Preparation time **10 minutes**
Cooking time **15–20 minutes**

6 ripe **figs**, halved
1 **cinnamon stick**, broken
   in half
2 tablespoons **agave nectar**
2 tablespoons **brandy**
1 cup **raspberries**
finely grated zest of 1 **orange**
⅔ cup **plain soy yogurt**

Arrange the fig halves, cut side up, in a baking dish with the cinnamon. Drizzle with 1 tablespoon of the agave nectar and the brandy.

Bake in a preheated oven, at 375°F, for 15–20 minutes, until soft. Sprinkle with the raspberries and turn to coat in the juices, then leave to cool slightly.

Mix the remaining agave nectar with the orange zest and soy yogurt and serve with the figs and raspberries.

For spiced fig & orange tarte tatin, heat
2 tablespoons agave nectar in a round flameproof, ovenproof dish on the stove. Add ½ teaspoon ground cinnamon and the finely grated zest of 1 orange and stir to mix, then place 6 halved ripe figs, cut side down, in the dish. Cover with a sheet of ready-to-use vegan puff pastry, tucking in the edges. Bake in a preheated oven, at 400°F, for 25–30 minutes, until well risen and golden. Carefully invert the dish onto a plate with a rim to catch the juices. Serve warm with plain soy yogurt or vegan ice cream.

vanilla-spiced fruit salad

Serves **4**

Preparation time **10 minutes**,
   plus cooling

Cooking time **8 minutes**

⅔ cup **apple juice**

1 **vanilla bean**, slit in half
   lengthwise

2 tablespoons **agave nectar**
   or packed **light brown sugar**

2 **kiwifruit**, peeled and sliced

1⅔ cups shulled and thickly
   sliced **strawberries**

1 cup **blueberries**

1 ripe **mango**, peeled, pitted,
   and sliced

mint leaves, to decorate

Warm the apple juice in a small saucepan with the split vanilla bean and agave nectar or sugar over gentle heat. Simmer gently for 4–5 minutes, then let cool completely. Remove the vanilla bean and scrape the seeds into the light syrup.

Combine the fruits in a large bowl and drizzle with the vanilla-spiced syrup. Stir gently to coat, then spoon into serving bowls and sprinkle with mint leaves to decorate.

For Asian-style fruit salad, simmer ⅔ cup pineapple juice in a saucepan with 2 star anise, 1 tablespoon lime juice, 2 cloves, and the agave nectar as above. Let cool, then chill for 1 hour. Cut off the top and bottom of 1 small pineapple and slice off the skin. Cut the pineapple into quarters and remove the core from each quarter. Cut into slices and combine with 1 peeled, pitted, and sliced mango, 2 cups drained canned litchis, and 2 sliced carambola (star fruits) in a serving bowl. Pour the syrup over the fruit and serve.

coconut rice pudding

Serves **4**

Preparation time **15 minutes**

Cooking time 1½ **hours**

⅓ cup **jasmine** or **short-grain rice**

¼ cup **granulated sugar**

1⅔ cups **coconut milk**

1⅔ cups **water**

1 ripe **mango**, peeled, pitted, and chopped

finely grated zest and juice of 1 **lime**

Put the rice in a saucepan with the sugar, coconut milk, and measured water.

Bring the mixture to a boil, stirring, then pour into a shallow 6½-cup ovenproof dish. Bake in a preheated oven, at 300°F, for 1 hour 25 minutes, stirring occasionally, until the rice is tender and the liquid is absorbed.

Mix together the mango and lime zest and juice in a bowl and serve with the warm or cold rice pudding.

For coconut rice pudding brûlée, bring the rice, sugar, coconut milk, and water to a boil, stirring, as above, then let simmer on the stove, stirring occasionally, for 20 minutes, until the rice is tender and the liquid is absorbed. Spoon the mixture into individual heatproof dishes, level the surface, and let cool. Chill for 2–3 hours or overnight. Just before serving, sprinkle 1 tablespoon demerara or other raw sugar evenly over the surface of each dish. Place under a hot broiler or use a cook's blowtorch to melt and caramelize the sugar. Let cool for 10 minutes to harden the caramel before serving with chopped mango or rhubarb compote.

blueberry & pear slump

Serves **4**

Preparation time **20 minutes**

Cooking time **25–30 minutes**

2 large ripe **pears**, peeled,
  cored and chopped

1 ⅓ cups **blueberries**

⅓ cup **granulated sugar**

1 ⅓ cups **all-purpose flour**

1 teaspoon **baking powder**

½ cup **ground almonds**
  (almond meal)

2 tablespoons **vegan spread**,
  diced

⅔ cup **almond milk**

¼ cup **slivered almonds**

Divide the pears and blueberries among 4 large ramekins and sprinkle with 2 tablespoons of the sugar.

Sift together the flour and baking powder into a bowl and stir in the ground almonds and 2 tablespoons of the remaining sugar. Add the spread and rub in with your fingertips. Stir in the almond milk to make a sticky dough.

Dot small spoonfuls of the dough over the fruit and sprinkle with the remaining 1 tablespoon sugar and the slivered almonds. Bake in a preheated oven, at 375°F, for 25–30 minutes, until the fruit is soft and the topping is golden.

For rhubarb, plum & orange slump, chop 5 rhubarb stalks and 4 plums and divide among 4 large ramekins. Sprinkle with 2 tablespoons granulated sugar. Sift 1⅔ cups all-purpose flour and 2 teaspoons baking powder together into a bowl and stir in ½ cup ground almonds (almond meal), 2 tablespoons granulated sugar, and the finely grated zest of 1 orange. Rub in 2 tablespoons diced vegan spread with the fingertips, then stir in 1 cup almond milk to make a soft dough. Dot spoonfuls of the mixture over the fruit and sprinkle with 1 tablespoon granulated sugar and ¼ cup slivered almonds. Bake as above.

poached peaches & raspberries

Serves **6**
Preparation time **15 minutes**
Cooking time **25 minutes**

1 cup **water**
⅔ cup **medium red wine**
 or **sweet sherry**
⅓ cup **granulated sugar**
1 **vanilla bean**
6 ripe **peaches**, halved and
 pitted
1 cup **raspberries**

Pour the measured water and red wine or sherry into a saucepan and add the sugar. Slit the vanilla bean in half lengthwise and scrape out the seeds into the pan, then add the bean. Heat gently until the sugar is dissolved.

Arrange the peach halves, cut side up, in an ovenproof dish so that they sit together snugly. Pour the hot syrup over them, then cover and cook in a preheated oven, at 350°F, for 20 minutes.

Sprinkle with the raspberries and serve the fruit either warm or cold. Spoon into serving bowls and decorate with the vanilla bean cut into thin strips.

For poached prunes with vanilla, make the sugar syrup as above, then add 2 cups pitted prunes instead of the peaches. Cover and simmer as above, then serve with spoonfuls of plain soy yogurt or cream and 4 crumbled vegan cookies.

apple with salted caramel sauce

Serves **4**
Preparation **5 minutes**
Cooking time **15 minutes**

¼ cup **vegan spread**
4 **crisp, sweet apples**,
  quartered, cored, and sliced
¼ cup firmly packed **light
  brown sugar**
2 pitted fresh **Medjool dates**,
  chopped
½ cup **vegan cream**
2 tablespoons **cold water**
½ teaspoon **sea salt flakes**

Melt the spread in a skillet, add the apples, and cook over medium heat for 2 minutes, until starting to soften.

Add the sugar and stir until melted. Add the dates, toss, and cook for a few seconds. Pour in the vegan cream and cook, stirring constantly, for 2 minutes to make a caramel sauce.

Stir in the measured cold water and heat over low heat until the sauce is smooth, then add the salt flakes and mix well. Serve warm with vegan cream or ice cream.

For caramel apple oatmeal crisp, soften the apples, omitting the dates, and make the caramel sauce as above, then spoon into an ovenproof dish. Melt ⅓ cup vegan spread with ⅓ cup demerara or other raw sugar and 1 tablespoon light corn syrup in a saucepan. Add 1¼ cups rolled oats, ⅓ cup all-purpose flour, and ¼ teaspoon baking powder, and stir well, then spoon the topping over the apples and caramel. Bake in a preheated oven, at 350°F, for 25–30 minutes, until golden.

banana fritters & cinnamon sugar

Serves **4**

Preparation time **20 minutes**, plus standing

Cooking time **5 minutes**

1¾ cups **all-purpose flour**
½ teaspoon **ground nutmeg**
2 teaspoons **ground cinnamon**
1½ cups **sparkling water**
sunflower oil, for deep-frying
4 **bananas**, halved both lengthwise and widthwise
3 tablespoons **demerara** or **other raw sugar**
1 tablespoon **granulated sugar**

Mix together the flour, nutmeg, and 1 teaspoon of the cinnamon in a bowl, then make a well in the center. Gradually add and beat in enough of the sparkling water to make a smooth batter thick enough to coat the back of a spoon. Let stand for 20 minutes.

Fill a deep saucepan one-third full with oil and heat to 350–375°F, or until a cube of bread browns in 30 seconds. Using a pair of tongs, dip the banana pieces, in batches, into the batter, gently lower into the hot oil, and cook for 30 seconds–1 minute, until golden and crisp, being careful not to overcrowd the pan with too many at a time, because they will stick together and the oil temperature will drop. Remove from the pan with a slotted spoon and drain on paper towels.

Mix the sugars with the cinnamon, then sprinkle it over the hot fritters to serve.

For apple & pear fritters with spiced sugar, make the batter and let stand as above. Peel, core, and quarter 3 crisp, sweet apples and 2 pears. Heat the oil as above. Using a pair of tongs, dip the apple and pear pieces, in batches, into the batter, gently lower into the hot oil and cook for 2 minutes, until golden. Remove from the pan with a slotted spoon and drain on paper towels. Mix ⅓ cup granulated sugar with 1 teaspoon ground cinnamon and ½ teaspoon ground allspice, then sprinkle it over the hot fritters to serve.

papaya with tumbling berries

Serves **4**

Preparation time **10 minutes**

2 large ripe **papayas**

1 cup **blueberries**

1 cup **raspberries**

1⅔ cups sliced and hulled **strawberries**

1 cup pitted **cherries** (optional)

agave syrup, to taste (optional)

lime wedges, to serve

Cut the papayas in half and scoop out the seeds and discard. Place each half on a serving plate.

Mix together the blueberries, raspberries, strawberries, and cherries, if using, in a bowl and then pile into the papaya halves.

Drizzle with a little agave syrup, if desired, and serve with lime wedges.

For papaya & berry smoothie, peel and halve 2 large ripe papayas, then remove and discard the seeds and cut the flesh into chunks. Put in a blender or food processor with the remaining fruits as above and 10 ice cubes. Add 2 cups apple or guava juice and blend until smooth. Pour into glasses and serve immediately.

champagne & raspberry gelatins

Serves **4**

Preparation time **15 minutes**, plus standing, cooling, and chilling

Cooking time **5 minutes**

1 cup **Champagne**

1¾ teaspoons **agar powder**

⅔ cup **apple and raspberry juice**

1 tablespoon **granulated sugar**

⅔ cup **raspberries**

mint sprigs, to decorate (optional)

Pour the Champagne into a small bowl, sprinkle with the agar powder, and set aside to dissolve.

Heat the apple and raspberry juice and sugar in a small saucepan and bring to a boil. Remove from the heat, then pour over the agar powder mixture and mix well. Let cool for 20 minutes.

Divide the raspberries among 4 glasses and pour the Champagne and juice mixture over the fruit. Refrigerate for 3–4 hours or overnight until set. Serve with a thin layer of soy cream on the top, if desired, although these gelatins are really refreshing served with just a sprig of mint.

For spiced cranberry gelatins, put 1¼ cups cranberry juice in a small saucepan with a broken cinnamon stick and bring to a boil. Remove from the heat and let steep until cool and the flavors develop. Meanwhile, sprinkle a 1½ teaspoons agar powder over ¼ cup of additional cranberry juice and set aside for 5 minutes to dissolve. Once the spiced cranberry juice is cool enough to touch, remove the cinnamon, pour the agar powder mixture over it, and mix well. Divide ½ cup cranberries among 4 glasses, pour the cranberry juice mixture over them, and refrigerate for 3–4 hours or overnight until set.

ultra-rich chocolate stacks

Serves **4**

Preparation time **20 minutes**, plus chilling

5 oz **semisweet chocolate**, broken into pieces

½ cup **coconut cream**

1 tablespoon **mint leaves**

1 cup **raspberries**

½ teaspoon **unsweetened cocoa powder**

½ teaspoon **confectioners' sugar**

Put the chocolate pieces in a heatproof bowl and set over a saucepan of hot water. Stir until melted.

Spoon 12 spoonfuls of the melted chocolate onto a baking sheet lined with parchment paper and let spread into about 3 inch disks, then refrigerate for 30 minutes, until set.

Whip the coconut cream in a bowl until thick. Layer 3 chocolate disks on each of 4 serving plates with the coconut cream, mint leaves, and raspberries.

Mix the cocoa and confectioners' sugar together, then dredge over the chocolate stacks to serve.

For chocolate & orange stacks, melt the chocolate as above, then stir in the finely grated zest of 1 orange. Spoon onto a lined baking sheet and refrigerate until set as above. Whip the coconut cream as above, then use to layer the disks in stacks of 3 along with 1 well-drained (11 oz) can mandarin segments in juice. Dredge with unsweetened cocoa powder to serve.

stuffed spiced roasted pears

Serves **4**

Preparation time **20 minutes**

Cooking time **35 minutes**

4 ripe **pears**, preferably a pale-
skinned variety

3 **pitted prunes**, coarsely
chopped

¼ cup roasted **hazelnuts,**
coarsely chopped

½ cup **blackberries,** halved

½ teaspoon **ground
cinnamon**

¼ cup **maple syrup**

2 tablespoons **vegan spread**

Halve the pears and then remove a small slice from the back of each so that they sit level in a roasting pan. Scoop out the core and seeds, leaving the stem intact.

Mix the prunes and hazelnuts with the cinnamon and maple syrup in a bowl, then fold in the blackberries. Pile into the pear cavities and top each with a small pat of the vegan spread. Cover the roasting pan with aluminum foil and bake in a preheated oven, at 400°F, for 25 minutes.

Remove the foil and roast for another 10 minutes. Serve with the juices spooned over the pears along with a scoop of soy ice cream or yogurt, if liked.

For stuffed roasted apples with agave syrup, peel 4 apples, cut each in half, and scoop out the core, leaving the stem intact. Remove a small slice from the back of each apple half so that it sits level in a roasting pan. Mix 2 coarsely chopped dried figs and ¼ cup lightly roasted almonds with ¼ cup agave syrup in a bowl, then fold in ⅓ cup raspberries. Spoon into the apple cavities and cover the pan with aluminum foil. Bake and then serve as above.

index

acknowledgments

Executive editor: Eleanor Maxfield
Text editor: Jo Richardson
Art direction and design: Penny Stock
Photographer: William Shaw
Home economist: Emma Frost
Stylist: Kim Sullivan
Production controller: Sarah Kramer

Photography copyright © Octopus Publishing Group Limited/William Shaw, except the following: copyright © Octopus Publishing Group/Stephen Conroy 73; Will Heap 91, 103, 209, 221; William Lingwood 97; William Reavell 63, 69; Ian Wallace 133, 139, 147, 171, 173.